The Ocean's Greatest Mysteries: Lost Ships and Hidden Treasures

Anam Rasheed

Published by Anam Rasheed, 2024.

THE OCEAN'S GREATEST MYSTERIES: LOST SHIPS AND HIDDEN TREASURES

First edition. October 9, 2024.

Copyright © 2024 Anam Rasheed.

ISBN: 979-8227378064

Written by Anam Rasheed.

Table of Contents

Prologue..1

Chapter 1: Vanished in the Bermuda Triangle..................2

Chapter 2: The Hunt for Blackbeard's Treasure................5

Chapter 3: Mysteries of the Mary Celeste.........................9

Chapter 4: Legends of Atlantis Beneath the Waves.......13

Chapter 5: Ghost Ship of the Arctic Sea.........................18

Chapter 6: The Sunken City of Dwarka...........................23

Chapter 7: The Secret of the Flying Dutchman..............28

Chapter 8: Searching for the Lost Gold of the Flor de la Mar......33

Chapter 9: Pirate Ships of the Caribbean.......................38

Chapter 10: The Disappearance of the USS Cyclops......44

Chapter 11: Treasures of the Deep Mediterranean........49

Chapter 12: The Mystery of the Titanic's Sister Ship....55

Chapter 13: The Sunken Silver of the San José...............60

Chapter 14: Lost Ships of the Ancient Romans.............65

Chapter 15: The Enigma of the Japanese Submarine I-52...........70

Chapter 16: The Hidden Gold of the Merchant Royal.............75

Chapter 17: The Shipwrecks of Cape Horn......................80

Chapter 18: The Curse of the Nuestra Señora de Atocha.............86

Chapter 19: The Mystery of the SS Waratah....................91

Chapter 20: Unsolved Secrets of the Ocean Depths........96

Epilogue... 102

Prologue

The ocean is a place of wonder and mystery, stretching across our world like a blanket of blue. It holds secrets that have fascinated explorers, adventurers, and dreamers for centuries. Beneath its surface lies a hidden world filled with ancient shipwrecks, lost treasures, and untold stories that have disappeared into the depths. Some say the ocean never forgets, that it holds onto the secrets of time, waiting for someone brave enough to uncover them.

In this book, we will dive deep into the ocean's greatest mysteries, uncovering stories of legendary ships that vanished without a trace, treasures that slipped into the sea, and eerie ghost ships that still drift upon the waves. From the warm waters of the Caribbean, where pirate ships once roamed, to the icy Arctic seas, where ships met their frozen fate, each chapter will reveal a new mystery. Some tales are shrouded in myth, while others are rooted in history—waiting for young explorers like you to learn and imagine.

So, grab your compass, put on your captain's hat, and prepare for an adventure across the seven seas. The ocean is calling, and it's time to set sail on a journey filled with wonders, mysteries, and the thrill of the unknown. Who knows, maybe one day, you'll be the one to discover a lost treasure or solve one of the great oceanic puzzles that has left even the greatest explorers puzzled for centuries.

Welcome aboard, young adventurer. Let's explore the ocean's greatest mysteries together!

Chapter 1: Vanished in the Bermuda Triangle

The Bermuda Triangle is one of the most mysterious places on Earth, and many people have disappeared there without a trace. It's a region in the Atlantic Ocean, shaped like a triangle, with its points located in Miami, Bermuda, and Puerto Rico. Over the years, hundreds of ships and planes have gone missing in this area, leading to all sorts of strange stories and theories about what might be happening.

One of the most famous disappearances happened in 1945, when five U.S. Navy planes, known as Flight 19, took off on a routine training mission. The weather was clear, and everything seemed normal. But soon after they entered the Bermuda Triangle, the planes started experiencing trouble. The pilots reported that their instruments weren't working properly and that they couldn't tell where they were. Radio communications grew more and more confused until they suddenly went silent. The planes, along with 14 crew members, vanished without a trace. To make things even stranger, a search plane sent to find them also disappeared. To this day, no wreckage from any of the planes has ever been found.

The mystery of the Bermuda Triangle has fascinated people for a long time, and many wonder why so many ships and planes vanish there. Some think that natural forces are to blame. The Bermuda Triangle is known for its unpredictable weather. Huge storms can pop up without warning, creating massive waves or strong winds that could easily overwhelm a ship or plane. There are also powerful ocean currents in the area, including something called the Gulf Stream, which moves quickly and could easily pull a ship off course. These natural factors could explain why some vessels get lost.

Another explanation involves something called magnetic anomalies. The Earth's magnetic field helps guide ships and planes by allowing them to use compasses to figure out which direction they're going. But in the Bermuda Triangle, strange magnetic fields may cause compasses to malfunction, leading pilots and captains in the wrong direction. If they lose their bearings, they could get hopelessly lost and run out of fuel or crash into the ocean.

But not everyone believes that natural forces are the only explanation. Some people think that something much stranger is going on in the Bermuda Triangle. One theory is that alien spacecraft might be involved. Some believe that extraterrestrial beings could be responsible for the disappearances, abducting people and ships for unknown reasons. Others think that the Bermuda Triangle might be home to an underwater base for these mysterious visitors from another world.

Another theory is that the lost city of Atlantis is involved. Atlantis is a legendary island that was said to have sunk beneath the ocean thousands of years ago. Some believe that powerful technology from Atlantis could still be active under the sea, creating disturbances that cause ships and planes to disappear. According to this theory, the energy left behind by the ancient civilization might still be powerful enough to mess with modern technology, causing strange events in the Bermuda Triangle.

Some people even suggest that time warps or portals might exist in the Bermuda Triangle. These could be like invisible doors in space and time, where a ship or plane could accidentally pass through and get stuck in another dimension or time period. Imagine flying into the Bermuda Triangle and suddenly being transported to another time in history, or even to another world altogether! This idea is a bit like science fiction, but it's fun to think about.

Despite all these theories, there is still no definite answer to what happens in the Bermuda Triangle. Many of the disappearances remain unsolved, with no wreckage or clues left behind. Some scientists believe that there's nothing special about the Bermuda Triangle at all. They point out that other parts of the world also have storms and tricky navigation problems, and ships and planes disappear in those places too. According to this view, the Bermuda Triangle might just have a bad reputation, and the disappearances are simply accidents caused by natural factors.

However, the mystery continues to capture the imagination of people all over the world. Some believe that new technology, like advanced underwater robots or satellite imaging, might eventually help us uncover the secrets of the Bermuda Triangle. Maybe one day, we'll find out exactly what happened to Flight 19 and the other ships and planes that vanished there. But until then, the Bermuda Triangle remains one of the ocean's greatest unsolved mysteries, leaving plenty of room for wonder and wild imagination.

No matter what the true cause of these vanishings is, the stories of the Bermuda Triangle remind us just how vast and mysterious the ocean can be. We've explored only a small fraction of the sea, and there's so much we don't know about what lies beneath the waves. Whether it's powerful storms, strange magnetic fields, alien visitors, or lost cities, the Bermuda Triangle will continue to be a place where anything seems possible. For as long as people sail the seas and fly the skies, they'll keep wondering what really happens in this mysterious part of the world. The ocean holds many secrets, and the Bermuda Triangle is just one of the most fascinating.

Chapter 2: The Hunt for Blackbeard's Treasure

Blackbeard, one of the most famous pirates in history, has captured the imaginations of people for centuries. His real name was Edward Teach, and he was known for being a fearsome and cunning pirate who ruled the seas in the early 1700s. Blackbeard's ship, the Queen Anne's Revenge, became the stuff of legend as he and his crew raided ships along the eastern coast of North America and the Caribbean, stealing gold, silver, and other valuable goods. But what really makes Blackbeard's story exciting is the idea that somewhere, hidden away, is a treasure so huge that it has never been found.

The story of Blackbeard's treasure begins with his reign of terror on the high seas. Blackbeard didn't just attack ships for the fun of it—he was after loot, and lots of it. Pirates like Blackbeard would capture merchant ships carrying valuable goods from Europe and the Americas, including gold coins, silver bars, spices, silks, and jewels. It's believed that Blackbeard and his crew amassed a fortune during their time, and much of it was hidden away in secret locations, waiting to be discovered.

Blackbeard was incredibly clever and knew how to outsmart the authorities who were trying to catch him. He was also known for his terrifying appearance, with a long black beard that he would sometimes tie with ribbons or light on fire to frighten his enemies. His reputation as a ruthless pirate only grew over time, and people began to believe that he had hidden his treasure in a place so secret that no one would ever find it.

One of the most intriguing parts of the story is that Blackbeard was thought to have buried his treasure before his death in 1718. After years of plundering and looting, Blackbeard's luck finally ran out when he was killed in a fierce battle with the British Navy off the coast of North

Carolina. According to legend, before his final battle, Blackbeard had buried a vast amount of gold and jewels somewhere on a remote island or hidden deep in a cave. However, before he could reveal the location of his treasure, he was captured and beheaded. His body was thrown overboard, and his head was placed on a pole as a warning to other pirates. With Blackbeard gone, his treasure was lost—if it ever existed at all.

For centuries, treasure hunters, historians, and adventurers have been on the hunt for Blackbeard's lost treasure. One of the main places people believe it could be hidden is in the Outer Banks of North Carolina, where Blackbeard spent a lot of time and was ultimately killed. The Outer Banks are a series of small islands along the coast, full of hidden coves, dense forests, and deep waters—perfect for a pirate looking to stash a fortune. People have explored these areas, hoping to uncover gold coins or treasure chests buried under the sand, but no one has ever found any solid proof of Blackbeard's treasure.

Another popular theory is that Blackbeard's treasure might be hidden in the Caribbean, where he carried out many of his raids. The Caribbean was a haven for pirates during Blackbeard's time, and there are countless small islands and caves that could have been used as secret hideouts. Some treasure hunters believe that Blackbeard might have buried his loot on one of these islands, possibly in the Bahamas or near Jamaica, but the exact location remains a mystery.

In 1996, a team of marine archaeologists made an exciting discovery that they believed could bring them closer to finding Blackbeard's treasure. Off the coast of North Carolina, near Beaufort, they found the wreck of what they believe to be Blackbeard's flagship, the Queen Anne's Revenge. The ship had been lost for nearly 300 years, and the discovery sent waves of excitement through the world of archaeology and pirate enthusiasts. Divers began exploring the wreck, finding cannons, anchors, and other artifacts from Blackbeard's time. However, while the ship was full of interesting historical items, there was no treasure found aboard. It seemed that if Blackbeard's treasure existed, it wasn't on the Queen Anne's Revenge.

Even though no treasure has been found yet, the search for Blackbeard's hidden fortune continues. There are many stories and clues that have kept people searching for over 300 years. Some believe that Blackbeard left behind cryptic messages or maps that point to the location of his treasure, but if such maps exist, no one has been able to crack the code. Others think that the treasure may have been moved or taken by members of Blackbeard's crew after his death. It's possible that only a few trusted pirates knew where the loot was buried, and they took the secret to their graves.

What makes the hunt for Blackbeard's treasure so fascinating is the mystery that surrounds it. Some people think that the treasure is still out there, waiting to be found by the right person at the right time. Others believe that the treasure might be nothing more than a myth, a story created by sailors and adventurers to keep Blackbeard's legend alive. After all, there's no concrete evidence that Blackbeard ever buried a treasure in the first place. But the idea that there could be a hidden fortune somewhere, filled with gold coins, glittering jewels, and pirate booty, is too tempting to ignore.

Pirates like Blackbeard have always been larger-than-life figures, and their stories are filled with danger, adventure, and treasure. Even though the chances of finding Blackbeard's treasure may be slim, the search itself is an exciting adventure. People who look for lost treasure often say that it's not just about the gold and riches—it's about the thrill of the hunt and the possibility that you might uncover something incredible. The ocean is full of secrets, and many of them are waiting to be discovered.

Even today, with modern technology like underwater robots and advanced sonar, the ocean can still hide its treasures. There are countless shipwrecks scattered across the ocean floor, and some of them might still hold treasure that was lost centuries ago. Blackbeard's treasure could be one of these hidden riches, or it could be buried deep in the sand on a remote island, waiting for someone brave enough to find it. The mystery keeps the legend of Blackbeard alive, and as long as people are drawn to the idea of pirates and treasure, the hunt will continue.

The idea of finding Blackbeard's treasure is a dream for many people, young and old. It's a reminder that the world is still full of mysteries and that there are still places left to explore. Whether or not the treasure is ever found, Blackbeard's story will always be part of pirate lore. His name will forever be linked to the excitement of the open seas, the danger of pirate life, and the thrill of searching for buried treasure. The hunt for Blackbeard's treasure may never end, and that's part of what makes it so magical. It invites everyone to imagine what it would be like to discover a chest full of gold coins, sparkling gems, and ancient pirate relics, hidden away by one of history's most infamous pirates.

Chapter 3: Mysteries of the Mary Celeste

The mystery of the Mary Celeste is one of the strangest and most puzzling stories from the sea. The Mary Celeste was a ship that was found drifting in the Atlantic Ocean in 1872, completely abandoned. The ship was in good condition, the cargo was still on board, and there was no sign of a struggle. Yet the crew had vanished, and no one has ever figured out exactly what happened to them. This mystery has fascinated people for over a century, and there are many theories about what could have caused the crew to disappear.

The Mary Celeste was a small ship, about 100 feet long, and it was built to carry cargo across the ocean. On November 7, 1872, the ship set sail from New York City, bound for Genoa, Italy. There were 10 people on board: the captain, Benjamin Briggs, his wife Sarah, their two-year-old daughter Sophia, and seven experienced crew members. The ship was carrying a cargo of industrial alcohol, which was being shipped to Europe. Everything seemed normal as they sailed out of the harbor and into the Atlantic.

However, just a few weeks later, on December 5, 1872, the Mary Celeste was found adrift in the middle of the ocean by a British ship called the Dei Gratia. When the crew of the Dei Gratia spotted the Mary Celeste, they immediately knew something was wrong. The ship was moving slowly, as if it had no one to guide it. When they boarded the ship, they found it completely deserted. The sails were partly set, and the ship was seaworthy, meaning it wasn't damaged or sinking. The cargo of alcohol was still in the hold, and there were six months' worth of food and water on board. But the lifeboat was missing, and the captain's logbook, which recorded the ship's journey, had stopped a week earlier.

The crew of the Dei Gratia was baffled. Where had the people on the Mary Celeste gone? There were no signs of violence or foul play. There was no evidence of a storm, and the ship was in good shape, so it didn't look like the crew had abandoned it in an emergency. The personal belongings of the crew were still in their cabins, and even valuable items, like the captain's sword and family possessions, were left behind. It was as if the people on the ship had vanished into thin air.

This strange discovery sparked one of the greatest maritime mysteries in history. Since the day the Mary Celeste was found, people have tried to figure out what happened to the crew, but no one knows for sure. There are many theories, some of them based on real possibilities, and others more wild and imaginative. Let's take a look at some of these ideas.

One theory is that the crew might have been poisoned by the alcohol fumes. The cargo of the Mary Celeste was made up of barrels of industrial alcohol, which is much stronger than the alcohol people drink. Some have suggested that the barrels might have leaked, causing dangerous fumes to build up inside the ship. If the crew smelled the fumes, they might have thought the ship was about to explode and rushed to abandon ship in the lifeboat. However, this theory doesn't explain why they would leave the ship so suddenly and not take more supplies or return when the ship didn't explode. Plus, when the ship was found, most of the barrels were still intact, and there was no sign of a leak.

Another idea is that the crew might have been caught in a sudden seaquake, or underwater earthquake. A seaquake could have rocked the ship violently, throwing the crew off balance and making them fear the ship was about to sink. If the seaquake caused strange waves or water disturbances, the crew might have panicked and taken the lifeboat to escape what they thought was a sinking ship. But again, the ship wasn't damaged, and there was no sign that it had been through a disaster like that.

Some people believe that piracy might have been involved. Pirates were common during that time, and there are stories of pirates attacking ships and taking the crew or forcing them off their ship.

However, in the case of the Mary Celeste, this theory doesn't seem to fit. Pirates usually stole valuable items, but nothing was missing from the ship. The cargo, the crew's belongings, and even the food and water were untouched. It seems unlikely that pirates would attack a ship, leave all the loot behind, and take only the people.

Then, there's the possibility that something went wrong with the ship's navigation or equipment. The captain of the Mary Celeste might have miscalculated their location or believed they were in danger from bad weather. If the captain thought the ship was about to hit rocks or be caught in a storm, he might have ordered everyone into the lifeboat to wait for help or to try to reach land. But this still doesn't explain why the crew didn't return to the ship when they realized it was safe.

One of the more supernatural theories involves sea monsters or aliens. Some people suggest that the crew might have been taken by a giant sea creature, like a kraken, or even abducted by aliens. While these ideas are fun to think about, there's no evidence to support them. There were no signs of a struggle or anything unusual on the ship, making these theories more of a product of the imagination than of reality.

Another possibility is mutiny. A mutiny happens when the crew of a ship rebels against the captain, often because they are unhappy or scared. Some people think that the crew of the Mary Celeste might have turned against Captain Briggs, perhaps because they were afraid of the dangerous cargo of alcohol. They might have forced him and his family into the lifeboat, then sailed away, only to have something go wrong. But the crew of the Mary Celeste was carefully chosen by the captain, and they were known to be loyal and experienced sailors. It's hard to imagine such a mutiny happening with no signs of violence on the ship.

There's also the theory that the crew might have been swept overboard by a rogue wave. A rogue wave is a massive, unexpected wave that can appear suddenly and is powerful enough to wash people overboard. If such a wave hit the Mary Celeste, it might have knocked the crew into the sea, leaving the ship empty. However, if this had happened, it's strange that no one would have tried to get back on the ship, especially with plenty of food and water still available.

Yet another idea is that the crew might have abandoned ship due to fear of a potential leak. Some researchers have suggested that the ship might have appeared to be taking on water, even though it wasn't sinking. If the crew saw water coming into the ship, they might have feared that it was going to sink and took to the lifeboat, thinking they were in immediate danger. However, the Mary Celeste was found in good condition, so if there had been a leak, it wasn't serious.

Despite all these theories, the mystery of the Mary Celeste remains unsolved. The ship itself was eventually taken to Genoa, where it continued to sail under different owners, but it never lost its eerie reputation as the "ghost ship" that had once been found abandoned in the middle of the ocean.

What really happened on the Mary Celeste? Did the crew abandon ship out of fear, or were they taken by some unseen force? Did they fall victim to a natural disaster, or did something more sinister occur? The truth may never be known, but the story of the Mary Celeste continues to capture the imagination of people around the world. It's a reminder that the sea can be full of mysteries, and sometimes, even the most experienced sailors can find themselves lost in the vastness of the ocean. The Mary Celeste remains one of the greatest unsolved maritime mysteries, a ghost ship whose secrets still drift across the waves, waiting for someone to uncover the truth.

Chapter 4: Legends of Atlantis Beneath the Waves

The legend of Atlantis is one of the most famous and enduring mysteries of the ancient world. Atlantis was said to be a powerful and advanced civilization that existed thousands of years ago, only to disappear beneath the ocean in a single, catastrophic event. The story of Atlantis comes from the writings of the ancient Greek philosopher Plato, who described the city as a great island empire that was wealthy, technologically advanced, and beautiful beyond imagination. According to Plato, Atlantis was a mighty naval power that had conquered much of the world before it was destroyed in a terrible disaster, leaving no trace behind. Ever since then, people have wondered if Atlantis was real, and if so, where it might be hidden beneath the waves.

The story of Atlantis first appeared in two of Plato's works, the *Timaeus* and the *Critias*, written around 360 BCE. Plato said that Atlantis was located beyond the "Pillars of Hercules," which we now know as the Strait of Gibraltar, the narrow passage between Spain and Morocco that leads from the Mediterranean Sea into the Atlantic Ocean. In Plato's tale, Atlantis was a vast island that existed about 9,000 years before his time, which would place it around 11,000 years ago. The island was ruled by a powerful king and was home to an advanced and wealthy society. Its people had great knowledge of science, engineering, and agriculture, and they built magnificent cities with towering temples, beautiful gardens, and huge harbors for their fleets of ships.

Atlantis was said to be a paradise, where the people enjoyed great prosperity, but over time, they became greedy and corrupt. According to Plato, the gods, angered by the people's wickedness, decided to punish them. In a single day and night, Atlantis was struck by a series of devastating earthquakes and floods, causing the entire island to sink beneath the sea, lost forever. Plato presented this story as a warning about the dangers of pride and greed, and it has been debated ever since whether Atlantis was based on a real place or if it was purely a myth created to teach a moral lesson.

Over the centuries, countless explorers, historians, and treasure hunters have searched for the lost city of Atlantis. People have looked for it all over the world, in places as far apart as the Mediterranean Sea, the Caribbean, and even Antarctica. One of the reasons Atlantis has remained so fascinating is that it could theoretically be anywhere, hidden beneath the ocean. The sea is so vast and largely unexplored that entire cities could be buried under the waves without us knowing it. The possibility that Atlantis is out there, waiting to be found, keeps the legend alive.

One of the most popular theories is that Atlantis might have been located on the island of Santorini, in the Aegean Sea. Santorini was once part of a large, circular island known as Thera, which was home to the Minoan civilization, one of the most advanced cultures of the ancient world. Around 1600 BCE, the island was destroyed by one of the largest volcanic eruptions in history. The eruption caused the island to collapse into the sea, creating a massive tidal wave, or tsunami, that devastated nearby areas. Some historians believe that this event could have inspired the story of Atlantis, especially since the Minoans were known for their advanced architecture and naval power, similar to the description of Atlantis.

Another theory suggests that Atlantis might have been located near the coast of Spain, in the region known as Andalusia. In recent years, some researchers have used satellite imagery to detect what appear to be ancient structures beneath the marshes of southern Spain, which some believe could be the ruins of Atlantis. This theory points out that the area was once prone to flooding and that a great civilization could have been destroyed by a massive flood or tsunami, just as Plato described.

Some people believe that Atlantis might have been located in the Caribbean, particularly around the islands of Cuba or the Bahamas. There have been claims of underwater structures and mysterious formations in these areas, such as the so-called "Bimini Road," a series of large stone blocks off the coast of the Bahama Islands that some think could be the remains of ancient Atlantean buildings. Others suggest that Atlantis could have been located in the Americas, with some even proposing that the city existed in what is now the Amazon rainforest or Mexico, where great civilizations like the Maya and Aztecs once thrived.

Another fascinating idea is that Atlantis might be hidden under the ice in Antarctica. Some theorists believe that Antarctica was once a temperate, inhabited land before a sudden shift in the Earth's crust caused it to move south, becoming covered in ice. According to this theory, the lost civilization of Atlantis could be buried beneath the ice sheets of Antarctica, waiting to be discovered. While there is no concrete evidence to support this idea, it captures the imagination because Antarctica is one of the most mysterious and least explored places on Earth.

The idea of a highly advanced civilization existing thousands of years ago has inspired many other theories about Atlantis. Some believe that the Atlanteans were not just technologically advanced but may have possessed knowledge far beyond what we understand today. According to some accounts, the people of Atlantis had developed advanced forms of energy, possibly using crystals or some other unknown technology to power their cities. They were thought to have great ships and even flying machines that allowed them to travel across the globe. Some legends suggest that the Atlanteans had contact with other ancient civilizations and that their knowledge may have been passed down to the Egyptians, the Mayans, or other cultures, helping to explain how these civilizations built their great pyramids and monuments.

There are also more mystical and imaginative ideas about Atlantis. Some believe that Atlantis was home to a race of beings with supernatural abilities, like telepathy, or even that they were descendants of extraterrestrial visitors. These ideas have been popularized in science fiction and fantasy stories, where Atlantis is often depicted as a lost world of advanced technology and ancient wisdom. In some versions of the story, the Atlanteans are said to have survived the destruction of their island and continued to live in secret, either beneath the ocean or in hidden places around the world, watching over humanity from afar.

Despite all the theories and searches, no one has ever found definitive proof of Atlantis. Some scholars believe that Atlantis was never a real place at all, but rather a fictional story created by Plato to illustrate his philosophical ideas. In Plato's writings, Atlantis represents a society that became corrupted by power and greed, and its destruction serves as a cautionary tale about the dangers of hubris. In this sense, the story of Atlantis might be more of an allegory than a historical account. Plato's tale was meant to show that even the greatest civilizations can fall if they lose their way, a message that has resonated throughout history.

Still, the allure of Atlantis persists, and the idea of a lost city beneath the waves continues to captivate people. The mystery of whether such a place really existed, and where it might be located, keeps adventurers and researchers intrigued. Some scientists believe that as our technology for exploring the ocean improves, we might one day find evidence of ancient cities lost beneath the sea. Already, discoveries of submerged ruins and ancient structures have been made in places like the Mediterranean and the Indian Ocean, suggesting that there are still many secrets to uncover in the depths of the ocean.

Whether Atlantis is ever found or not, the legend of the lost city remains one of the most fascinating and enduring myths of all time. It speaks to the human desire to explore the unknown, to search for answers, and to uncover the secrets of the past. Atlantis represents the possibility that there are still great mysteries in the world, waiting to be solved. It invites us to imagine a time when advanced civilizations flourished long before recorded history, and it reminds us that the ocean, with its vast, unexplored depths, may still hold treasures beyond our wildest dreams.

As long as people are drawn to stories of adventure and discovery, the legend of Atlantis will continue to inspire explorers, scholars, and dreamers alike. Whether it's a real place waiting to be found or a powerful symbol of human ambition and downfall, Atlantis will always have a special place in the world of myths and legends. The lost city beneath the waves may never be discovered, but the quest to find it will live on, keeping the mystery of Atlantis alive for generations to come.

Chapter 5: Ghost Ship of the Arctic Sea

The story of the *Ghost Ship of the Arctic Sea* is one of the most eerie and mysterious tales of the high seas. Imagine a ship drifting through the freezing waters of the Arctic, its sails torn and flapping in the icy wind. No one is at the helm, no crew is on deck, and there's not a single soul on board. The ship moves silently, carried by the currents, seemingly abandoned. Yet, the ship itself looks strangely preserved, almost as if its crew had only just vanished. This image has captured the imaginations of sailors and adventurers for centuries, and many wonder: what happened to the ghost ships of the Arctic, and why do these mysteries endure?

One of the most famous ghost ships of the Arctic is the *Octavius*, a ship that, according to legend, was discovered in 1775, drifting through the icy waters off the coast of Greenland. The crew of a whaling ship named the *Herald* spotted the *Octavius* and decided to board it to investigate. As they stepped aboard the deserted vessel, they were met with a chilling scene. The entire crew of the *Octavius* was still on board, but they were all dead, frozen solid in their positions, as if they had been instantly turned to ice. The captain was found at his desk, still holding a pen, with his logbook in front of him. It seemed as though time had simply stopped on the ship. The crew of the *Herald* quickly abandoned the *Octavius*, frightened by the sight of the frozen men and the ghostly silence that hung over the ship.

The logbook found on the *Octavius* told a strange and tragic tale. It revealed that the ship had left England in 1761, bound for China. After successfully reaching its destination, the captain had made the fateful decision to attempt to return to England by sailing through the treacherous Northwest Passage, a route through the Arctic that was, at the time, largely uncharted and incredibly dangerous. The *Octavius* had sailed into the Arctic, but it never made it back to England. The ship had become trapped in the ice, and the crew had frozen to death. For

14 years, the *Octavius* had been drifting through the Arctic, its crew preserved by the cold, until it was discovered by the crew of the *Herald*.

The tale of the *Octavius* is a ghostly one, and while some historians believe that it may be more of a legend than a true story, it reflects the very real dangers of sailing in the Arctic. During the Age of Exploration, many ships ventured into the icy waters of the North in search of new trade routes and riches, but the Arctic is an unforgiving place. The ice can trap a ship in a matter of hours, and the cold is so intense that anyone caught without proper protection can freeze to death in minutes. The isolation of the Arctic adds to the sense of danger. In the vast, icy wilderness, a ship could easily become lost, its crew cut off from any hope of rescue. This is what makes the stories of ghost ships in the Arctic so haunting – they are reminders of the many ships and sailors who disappeared into the frozen north, never to return.

Another famous ghost ship of the Arctic is the *SS Baychimo*, a ship that earned its title as a ghost ship by drifting through the Arctic, abandoned, for more than 30 years. The *Baychimo* was a steel-hulled cargo ship built in the early 20th century to transport furs and goods between Europe and Canada. In 1931, while on a routine trip along the coast of Alaska, the ship became trapped in ice near the town of Barrow (now known as Utqiaġvik), one of the northernmost inhabited places in the world.

At first, the crew of the *Baychimo* thought they would be able to free the ship from the ice, but as the days passed, it became clear that the ship was stuck fast. The crew set up a camp on the ice and waited for the weather to improve. After several weeks, a blizzard struck, and when the storm finally cleared, the crew was stunned to find that the *Baychimo* had vanished. Assuming the ship had broken free and sunk, the crew returned to Barrow, ready to head home. But just a few days later, a hunter spotted the *Baychimo* drifting about 45 miles away, still afloat.

The crew managed to reach the ship and retrieve some of the cargo, but the ice conditions were too dangerous to stay aboard, so they abandoned the *Baychimo*, leaving it to the Arctic sea. Over the years that followed, the *Baychimo* was spotted multiple times, drifting aimlessly through the Arctic waters. Sometimes it would be seen stuck in the ice, other times it would be floating freely. Various attempts were made to board the ship, but the treacherous conditions of the Arctic made it nearly impossible. Eventually, the *Baychimo* earned the nickname "The Ghost Ship of the Arctic" because it seemed to appear and disappear mysteriously, always just out of reach.

For decades, the *Baychimo* continued to drift, seemingly defying the odds. There were sightings of the ship as late as the 1960s, but after that, it was never seen again. To this day, the ultimate fate of the *Baychimo* remains unknown. Some believe that the ship finally sank beneath the icy waters, while others think it might still be drifting somewhere in the Arctic, waiting to be rediscovered.

The Arctic is a place of extreme conditions, and these stories of ghost ships highlight the dangers faced by those who dared to explore its icy waters. The combination of freezing temperatures, thick ice, and isolation creates an environment where a ship can easily become stranded, and where survival is often impossible. For those unlucky enough to become trapped in the Arctic, the cold can be a merciless killer, freezing everything and everyone in its path. Ships like the *Octavius* and the *Baychimo* became ghost ships not because of any supernatural force, but because the Arctic itself is so harsh and inhospitable that even the sturdiest vessels and most experienced sailors can be defeated by it.

But the idea of ghost ships in the Arctic also stirs the imagination. There is something haunting about the thought of a ship drifting through the ice, its crew long gone, but the ship itself still afloat, as if waiting for its final rest. These ships are like time capsules, frozen in time, carrying with them the stories of the men who sailed them and the dangers they faced. When a ship is found abandoned, with no sign of its crew, it raises questions that may never be answered. Did the crew perish in the cold, or were they forced to abandon the ship in a desperate bid for survival? Did they meet their end in the unforgiving Arctic wilderness, or did something else happen, something more mysterious?

In recent years, advances in technology have allowed explorers to probe deeper into the mysteries of the Arctic. Satellites and sonar equipment have helped locate shipwrecks that were lost for centuries, hidden beneath the ice. One of the most famous recent discoveries is that of the HMS *Erebus* and HMS *Terror*, two ships that were part of an expedition led by Sir John Franklin in 1845 to find the Northwest Passage. Franklin's expedition disappeared without a trace, and for more than 150 years, the fate of the ships and their crew was one of the greatest mysteries of Arctic exploration. In 2014, the wreck of the HMS *Erebus* was found in the Arctic, followed by the discovery of the HMS *Terror* in 2016. These discoveries have shed new light on what happened to Franklin's ill-fated expedition, but the full story is still being pieced together.

The Arctic continues to hold many secrets, and the stories of ghost ships like the *Octavius*, the *Baychimo*, and Franklin's ships remind us of the perils of exploring this remote and dangerous part of the world. For as long as humans have sailed the seas, the Arctic has been a place of wonder and terror, a frozen wilderness that can claim ships and men without a trace. The ghost ships of the Arctic are a haunting reminder of the risks taken by those who sought to conquer its icy waters, and they stand as symbols of the mysteries that still lie hidden in the cold, dark depths of the sea.

Even today, with all our modern technology, the Arctic remains a place of mystery. The vastness of the ocean and the uncharted regions of the Arctic make it possible that more ghost ships are out there, drifting through the ice, waiting to be discovered. These ships may hold the key to understanding more about the past, about the explorers who dared to sail into the unknown, and about the dangers they faced. The ghost ships of the Arctic are not just stories of the past – they are also a reminder that the ocean, and particularly the frozen waters of the far north, are still filled with unknowns, and that sometimes, even the most well-prepared explorers can fall victim to the unforgiving forces of nature.

Chapter 6: The Sunken City of Dwarka

The story of the Sunken City of Dwarka is one of the most fascinating and mysterious tales of ancient India. Dwarka is a city mentioned in Hindu mythology as the legendary kingdom of Lord Krishna, one of the most important and beloved deities in Hinduism. According to the ancient texts, Dwarka was a magnificent city, filled with grand palaces, temples, and gardens, and it was said to have been built by the god Vishwakarma, the architect of the gods, on the orders of Lord Krishna. The city was located on the coast of present-day Gujarat in western India, and it was known as a center of wealth, culture, and learning. However, as the legend goes, after Krishna left the Earth, Dwarka was submerged into the sea and lost forever.

For thousands of years, the Sunken City of Dwarka was thought to be just a myth, a part of the rich mythology of ancient India. The stories of Dwarka can be found in ancient Hindu scriptures like the *Mahabharata*, the *Bhagavata Purana*, and the *Harivamsa*, which describe it as a place of extraordinary beauty and prosperity. Krishna, who is often seen as an incarnation of the god Vishnu, is said to have ruled over Dwarka, and the city was described as being built of gold, silver, and precious gems. The people of Dwarka were skilled in trade, art, and science, and the city was home to many great scholars and warriors.

But, according to the legend, after the death of Krishna, Dwarka was fated to disappear. The gods decided that it was time for the city to return to the sea from which it had risen. As the story goes, the sea began to rise and swallow the city, slowly covering its streets and buildings with water. The people fled, and soon, the once-great city was lost beneath the waves. For centuries, Dwarka was thought to be nothing more than a mythical city, much like the legend of Atlantis in Greek mythology. It was a story passed down through generations, a part of India's cultural and religious heritage, but without any physical evidence to prove its existence.

However, in the 20th century, something incredible happened. Archaeologists and marine scientists began to explore the coastal waters off the coast of modern-day Dwarka, a city in the state of Gujarat that was believed to be the location of the ancient kingdom. In the 1960s, a team of researchers led by the Archaeological Survey of India (ASI) began underwater excavations near the coast. What they found shocked the world. Beneath the shallow waters of the Arabian Sea, they discovered the remains of an ancient city, complete with walls, pillars, and streets that appeared to match the descriptions of the legendary city of Dwarka.

The underwater ruins that were found included well-structured stone blocks, fortifications, and a series of walls and buildings that seemed to be part of a planned city. The discovery sparked great excitement and raised the possibility that the legendary city of Dwarka might not just be a myth after all. Further explorations were carried out, and more ruins were uncovered, including evidence of large stone anchors, which suggested that Dwarka had once been a major port city with a thriving maritime trade network.

One of the most amazing aspects of this discovery is that the ruins found beneath the sea near Dwarka date back thousands of years, possibly as far back as 1500 BCE or earlier. This places the city in a period that aligns with the ancient texts describing Lord Krishna's reign, leading many to believe that the ruins could indeed be the remains of the fabled city mentioned in the Hindu epics. The idea that a real city might have existed beneath the waves, and that it could be linked to the legendary city of Lord Krishna, captivated the imagination of people across the world.

The underwater city of Dwarka is believed to have been submerged by rising sea levels, which occurred over many centuries. Geological studies suggest that at the end of the last Ice Age, approximately 12,000 years ago, sea levels were much lower than they are today. As the Earth's climate warmed and the ice caps melted, sea levels gradually rose, and many coastal cities around the world were lost to the ocean. The city of Dwarka may have been one of these, submerged slowly over time as the waters of the Arabian Sea advanced inland.

The ruins found off the coast of modern Dwarka are spread over a vast area, covering several square kilometers, and they show evidence of a highly developed and well-planned city. The stone structures, walls, and streets suggest that the people who lived in Dwarka were skilled architects and engineers. Some of the ruins are as deep as 40 meters below the water, indicating that the city was gradually submerged over a long period. The layout of the city seems to match the descriptions found in ancient texts, with wide roads, grand public buildings, and large marketplaces.

One of the most important discoveries made during the underwater excavations was a set of massive stone anchors, which suggests that Dwarka was once a thriving port city with a bustling maritime trade. These anchors, some of which weigh several tons, were used to moor large ships, indicating that Dwarka was a hub for trade between India and other civilizations. This finding is significant because it shows that Dwarka was not only a legendary kingdom but also a real and prosperous city that played a key role in ancient Indian trade and commerce.

The discovery of the underwater city has also provided valuable insights into the history and culture of ancient India. The artifacts and ruins found at the site suggest that the people of Dwarka were highly advanced in terms of architecture, engineering, and maritime technology. The city was built with great precision, using large stone blocks that were carefully cut and fitted together, much like the construction techniques used in other ancient civilizations like Egypt and Mesopotamia. The presence of temples and religious structures also indicates that the people of Dwarka were deeply spiritual and that religion played an important role in their society.

While the ruins found underwater match many of the descriptions of the legendary city of Dwarka, there is still much debate among historians and archaeologists about whether these ruins are indeed the remains of the city mentioned in the ancient Hindu texts. Some scholars argue that the city found beneath the sea may be a different, unrelated ancient settlement, while others believe that the city of Dwarka could have been rebuilt several times over the centuries, with the ruins representing one of the later versions of the city. Nevertheless, the discovery of the underwater ruins has reignited interest in the legend of Dwarka and has given new life to the ancient stories of Lord Krishna and his kingdom.

The Sunken City of Dwarka is often compared to other legendary lost cities, such as Atlantis, which is said to have disappeared beneath the waves in a single day and night. Like Atlantis, Dwarka is a city that was once great and powerful, only to be lost to the sea. However, unlike Atlantis, which remains a mystery with no concrete evidence, Dwarka has left behind physical traces that suggest it was a real place. The discovery of Dwarka's ruins is a reminder that many of the world's greatest civilizations may lie hidden beneath the sea, waiting to be uncovered.

In recent years, advanced technology has allowed archaeologists to continue exploring the underwater ruins of Dwarka. Sonar mapping, underwater robots, and satellite imagery have all been used to create detailed maps of the submerged city, revealing new insights into its layout and construction. These technologies have allowed researchers to study the ruins in greater detail and to search for more clues about the history and fate of the city. The ongoing exploration of Dwarka is an exciting field of study, and many believe that more discoveries will be made in the future that could provide even more evidence about the city's origins and its connection to Lord Krishna.

The story of the Sunken City of Dwarka continues to inspire people all over the world. It is a tale of mystery, adventure, and wonder, combining elements of history, mythology, and science. For believers, Dwarka is a sacred place, linked to the life and legacy of Lord Krishna, and the discovery of the city's ruins is seen as proof of the truth of the ancient scriptures. For historians and archaeologists, Dwarka is a key to understanding the ancient civilizations of India and their connections to the wider world. And for dreamers and adventurers, the Sunken City of Dwarka is a reminder that there are still great mysteries waiting to be solved, hidden beneath the waves of the ocean.

The ocean holds many secrets, and the Sunken City of Dwarka is just one of the many lost civilizations that may be hidden beneath its depths. As exploration of the oceans continues, who knows what other ancient cities and forgotten kingdoms may be found? Perhaps one day, we will uncover the full story of Dwarka and learn more about the people who lived there, their culture, their beliefs, and their ultimate fate. Until then, the Sunken City of Dwarka remains one of the greatest mysteries of the ancient world, a symbol of the power and beauty of civilizations long gone but never forgotten.

Chapter 7: The Secret of the Flying Dutchman

The legend of the Flying Dutchman is one of the most famous and enduring sea myths in history. This ghostly tale has been told for hundreds of years, captivating the imaginations of sailors, storytellers, and adventurers. The Flying Dutchman is said to be a ghost ship that haunts the seas, particularly around the Cape of Good Hope at the southern tip of Africa. According to legend, the ship is cursed to sail the oceans forever, never reaching land, and any sailor who sees it is doomed to suffer terrible misfortune.

The story of the Flying Dutchman has many variations, but the most well-known version centers around a Dutch captain, often referred to as Captain Hendrik van der Decken, who was sailing his ship in the 17th century. The captain was known to be a skilled and fearless sailor, but he was also said to be stubborn, hot-tempered, and sometimes even reckless. The legend begins with van der Decken and his crew attempting to sail around the Cape of Good Hope, a dangerous and stormy route that had claimed the lives of many sailors before them.

As the Flying Dutchman neared the Cape, it was caught in a violent storm. The winds howled, the waves crashed against the ship, and the sky darkened as thunder and lightning raged overhead. The crew, terrified for their lives, begged the captain to turn back, but van der Decken refused. He was determined to complete the journey, no matter the cost. In his stubbornness, he is said to have made a fateful vow: "I will round this Cape, even if it takes me until Judgment Day!" With those words, he sealed his doom.

The storm grew fiercer, but van der Decken would not change course. According to the legend, his defiance angered the heavens, and as punishment, he and his ship were cursed to sail the seas forever, never able to make port or reach the safety of land. Some versions of the story say that an angel or the devil himself appeared to the captain, cursing him for his arrogance and dooming him and his crew to eternal wandering. From that moment on, the Flying Dutchman became a ghost ship, a spectral vessel with a crew of the damned, doomed to sail the oceans for all eternity.

For centuries, sailors have reported sightings of the Flying Dutchman. These reports often describe the ghostly ship appearing out of nowhere, sailing through rough seas with full sails, even when there is no wind. The ship is said to glow with an eerie light, and sometimes it is seen as a shadowy figure on the horizon, disappearing as mysteriously as it appeared. Some accounts say that the ship's sails are torn and ragged, and its crew are ghostly figures, sometimes seen waving or calling out, but their words are carried away by the wind.

One of the most famous recorded sightings of the Flying Dutchman took place in 1881, when Prince George of Wales, who later became King George V of England, was sailing off the coast of Australia as part of a naval training voyage. According to the prince's journal, the lookout on the ship spotted the Flying Dutchman in the early hours of the morning. The ghostly ship appeared in a strange red glow, and the sailors who saw it were filled with dread. The prince himself noted the sighting, describing how the phantom ship appeared and then vanished as suddenly as it had come. The lookout who first spotted the ship later fell to his death from the mast, further cementing the Flying Dutchman's reputation as a harbinger of doom.

Another famous sighting occurred in the early 20th century when the Flying Dutchman was reportedly seen off the coast of South Africa by several witnesses. The ship was said to have appeared out of a thick fog, sailing towards shore with full sails, but before it could reach the land, it disappeared. This sighting was widely reported in newspapers at the time, and it contributed to the growing legend of the ghost ship.

The Flying Dutchman has become a symbol of the mysterious and often deadly nature of the sea. For centuries, sailors have feared encountering the ship, believing that to see it was an omen of disaster. Many sailors who claimed to have seen the Flying Dutchman were later involved in shipwrecks or other misfortunes, and the legend grew that the ship was cursed to bring bad luck to anyone who saw it. Some say that the Flying Dutchman appears only during storms, while others claim that it can be seen in calm weather, silently gliding across the water like a shadow.

But what could be the truth behind the legend? Some historians and researchers believe that the story of the Flying Dutchman may have originated from real-life events. In the 17th and 18th centuries, sailing around the Cape of Good Hope was incredibly dangerous. The waters off the southern tip of Africa are some of the roughest in the world, with unpredictable storms, strong currents, and massive waves that could easily sink a ship. Many ships were lost in these waters, and it's possible that the legend of the Flying Dutchman began as a way to explain the disappearance of ships that never made it around the Cape.

In fact, the Cape of Good Hope was often called the "Cape of Storms" because of the treacherous conditions. It's possible that early sailors, witnessing the sudden appearance of a ship through the mist or fog, mistook it for a ghost ship, especially if they were already on edge due to the dangerous conditions. Over time, these sightings may have been embellished into the full-blown legend of a cursed ship that could never make it to port.

There are also natural phenomena that could help explain some of the sightings of the Flying Dutchman. One possible explanation is the "Fata Morgana" effect, a type of mirage that occurs when layers of air at different temperatures bend light in such a way that distant objects, like ships, can appear to float in the air or on the horizon. This optical illusion could make a ship seem to appear out of nowhere or give it an eerie, ghostly quality. Sailors seeing such an effect might have believed they were witnessing something supernatural.

However, even with these explanations, the legend of the Flying Dutchman has persisted. The story of a ship doomed to sail the seas forever, unable to find peace or safety, strikes a chord with many people, especially sailors who face the dangers of the ocean every day. The sea has always been a place of mystery, and the legend of the Flying Dutchman speaks to our deepest fears of the unknown and the uncontrollable forces of nature.

The Flying Dutchman has also found its way into popular culture. The story has inspired countless books, films, and songs, and the ghost ship has appeared in everything from operas to modern-day movies. One of the most famous cultural references to the Flying Dutchman is in the opera by the German composer Richard Wagner, titled *Der fliegende Holländer* (The Flying Dutchman). In Wagner's version of the story, the captain of the ghost ship is cursed to wander the seas until he can find a woman who will love him faithfully, thus breaking the curse. This romanticized version of the legend has become one of the most well-known interpretations of the tale.

The Flying Dutchman also plays a prominent role in the popular *Pirates of the Caribbean* film series, where it is portrayed as a ghost ship captained by Davy Jones, a supernatural being with control over the seas and the power to claim the souls of sailors who are lost at sea. In the films, the Flying Dutchman is depicted as a dark and fearsome ship, crewed by monstrous figures who are bound to the ship for eternity. This portrayal, while heavily fictionalized, has helped to keep the legend of the Flying Dutchman alive in the modern world.

Despite its fictional portrayals, the core of the Flying Dutchman legend remains the same: it is a story of a ship that defies the natural order, a vessel that continues to sail the seas long after it should have found rest. The idea of a ghost ship cursed to wander the oceans forever resonates with the ancient fears of sailors who faced the perils of the open sea, never knowing if they would return home. The Flying Dutchman represents the ultimate in maritime mystery – a ship that is both real and unreal, a symbol of the eternal dangers of the ocean.

Over the centuries, the Flying Dutchman has become more than just a maritime legend; it has become a symbol of the mysterious and powerful forces that rule the seas. The ship, doomed to sail forever without finding land, reminds us of the vastness and unpredictability of the ocean. In a time when sailors relied on little more than the stars to navigate, and when storms could sink even the sturdiest vessels, the sea was a place where the line between life and death was often blurred. The Flying Dutchman embodies this sense of danger and uncertainty, representing the unknown that lurks just beyond the horizon.

Even today, the legend of the Flying Dutchman continues to fascinate. While most people no longer fear the ship as a harbinger of doom, the idea of a ghostly vessel sailing through the mists remains a powerful and evocative image. Whether seen as a warning to those who would defy the sea or as a symbol of the mysteries that lie beneath the waves, the Flying Dutchman remains one of the most enduring and captivating stories of the sea.

As long as there are sailors brave enough to venture out onto the ocean, and as long as the sea continues to hold its secrets, the story of the Flying Dutchman will live on. It is a legend that has transcended time, evolving from a simple ghost story into a powerful myth about the forces of nature, the courage of sailors, and the mysteries of the deep. The Flying Dutchman may never find its final resting place, but its legend will continue to haunt the seas and the imaginations of those who hear its tale.

Chapter 8: Searching for the Lost Gold of the Flor de la Mar

The story of the lost gold of the *Flor de la Mar* is one of the greatest treasure mysteries of all time, filled with adventure, danger, and intrigue. The *Flor de la Mar*, which means "Flower of the Sea" in Portuguese, was a large Portuguese carrack, a type of ship used in the 16th century for long voyages across the oceans. It was one of the most famous ships of its era, and it became even more famous after it was lost at sea, along with a fortune in gold, silver, and jewels that has never been recovered.

The *Flor de la Mar* was built in 1502, and at the time, it was one of the largest ships in the Portuguese fleet. The Portuguese were one of the most powerful seafaring nations during the Age of Exploration, and their ships sailed all over the world, from Europe to Africa to Asia, in search of new trade routes, lands, and treasures. The *Flor de la Mar* was used to transport valuable goods like spices, silks, and precious metals back to Portugal from the Portuguese colonies in the East. It was known for its size, carrying capacity, and strength, but despite its grandeur, the ship had a troubled history.

From the beginning, the *Flor de la Mar* experienced difficulties. It was a massive ship for its time, and its size made it difficult to navigate in shallow waters. It had a tendency to leak, and over the years, it had been involved in several accidents and near shipwrecks. Nevertheless, the ship continued to be used for important missions because of its ability to carry vast amounts of cargo. By the early 1500s, the Portuguese had established a strong presence in the Indian Ocean, particularly in the region that is now Malaysia, Indonesia, and India. They were involved in trade and, at times, conflict with local kingdoms, and their ships were often filled with riches from these regions.

In 1511, the *Flor de la Mar* was involved in one of the most significant military campaigns of the Portuguese empire. Under the command of the famous Portuguese general Afonso de Albuquerque, the ship was part of a fleet sent to conquer the city of Malacca, which was one of the most important trading ports in Southeast Asia at the time. Malacca was a wealthy and powerful city, strategically located along the trade routes between China, India, and the Middle East. Whoever controlled Malacca controlled the flow of goods and riches through the region, and the Portuguese were determined to seize it.

Albuquerque successfully captured Malacca after a fierce battle, and the city's wealth became the spoils of war. The Portuguese soldiers and sailors plundered the city, taking gold, silver, jewels, and other treasures. Albuquerque himself acquired an enormous amount of wealth during the conquest. In addition to the treasure taken from Malacca, there were gifts and tributes sent by neighboring rulers who wanted to establish friendly relations with the Portuguese. This treasure, which was estimated to be one of the greatest fortunes ever amassed at the time, was loaded onto the *Flor de la Mar* for the journey back to Portugal.

The treasure included gold coins, bars of silver, pearls, precious gems like diamonds and rubies, and priceless artifacts from the region's royal palaces and temples. Some historians believe that the cargo of the *Flor de la Mar* may have included a treasure so vast and valuable that it would be worth billions of dollars in today's terms. The ship was supposed to carry this treasure back to Portugal, where it would become a symbol of the Portuguese empire's dominance and wealth.

However, the *Flor de la Mar* would never complete its journey. In November 1511, the ship set sail from Malacca, heavily loaded with treasure. It was commanded by Albuquerque himself, who was eager to return to Portugal with his immense fortune. The ship was accompanied by several other vessels in the fleet, and the plan was to sail across the Indian Ocean, rounding the Cape of Good Hope at the southern tip of Africa, and then head north to Europe.

But the seas around Southeast Asia were treacherous, filled with shallow reefs, hidden rocks, and unpredictable weather. As the *Flor de la Mar* sailed through the Strait of Malacca, it was hit by a powerful storm. The winds howled, the waves grew enormous, and the ship, already struggling because of its size and heavy load, began to break apart. Despite the best efforts of the crew, the ship was driven onto a reef off the coast of Sumatra, an island in present-day Indonesia.

The *Flor de la Mar* sank in the storm, taking with it nearly all of its crew and, of course, the treasure. Albuquerque and a few others managed to survive the shipwreck, escaping in a small boat. They made it to safety, but the ship and its precious cargo were lost forever beneath the waves. The exact location where the ship sank is unknown, but it is believed to be somewhere in the waters off the northern coast of Sumatra, near the present-day Aceh province.

Ever since the *Flor de la Mar* sank, treasure hunters, adventurers, and historians have been fascinated by the mystery of its lost fortune. The sheer value of the treasure, combined with the difficulty of locating the wreck, has made it one of the most sought-after lost treasures in history. Many expeditions have been launched to find the wreck of the *Flor de la Mar*, but none have been successful so far. The waters around Sumatra are dangerous, filled with reefs, strong currents, and unpredictable weather, making it difficult for modern-day explorers to search the area.

One of the reasons the treasure of the *Flor de la Mar* is so elusive is the fact that the ship sank in a region prone to strong ocean currents and seismic activity. Over the centuries, the shifting sands of the seabed, as well as underwater earthquakes, may have buried the wreck even deeper beneath the ocean floor. Some believe that the wreck may be in pieces, scattered over a wide area by storms and underwater movements, which makes it even more difficult to locate.

The search for the *Flor de la Mar* has drawn the attention of treasure hunters from around the world. Some have invested millions of dollars in state-of-the-art technology, using sonar, underwater robots, and satellite imagery to try to pinpoint the location of the wreck. But despite all these efforts, the treasure remains hidden. Some believe that the treasure may never be found, that it is lost forever, buried deep beneath the ocean floor or carried away by the strong currents of the Indian Ocean.

Others, however, remain hopeful that one day, the lost gold of the *Flor de la Mar* will be recovered. The allure of such an incredible fortune continues to inspire treasure hunters to brave the dangerous waters of the Sumatran coast in search of the shipwreck. The discovery of such a treasure would not only be one of the greatest finds in history but would also provide valuable insights into the early days of European exploration and the rise of the Portuguese empire.

But the story of the *Flor de la Mar* is not just about treasure; it is also a story of adventure and tragedy. The ship's sinking was a disaster for the Portuguese empire, which had hoped to use the wealth from Malacca to fund further explorations and conquests. For Albuquerque, the loss of the treasure was a personal blow, as he had risked his life and reputation to capture Malacca and claim its riches. Although he survived the shipwreck, Albuquerque was never able to recover from the loss of the *Flor de la Mar* and its treasure, and he died a few years later, leaving behind a legacy of both glory and failure.

The tale of the *Flor de la Mar* has also captured the imagination of writers, filmmakers, and storytellers. The image of a treasure-laden ship lost at sea, its gold and jewels lying untouched beneath the waves for centuries, has become a symbol of the enduring mystery and romance of the sea. Over the years, the legend of the lost gold of the *Flor de la Mar* has been woven into countless books, films, and TV shows about pirates, explorers, and treasure hunters.

Despite the many years that have passed since the ship sank, the mystery of the *Flor de la Mar* remains as intriguing as ever. The possibility that such a vast treasure could still be hidden somewhere beneath the ocean continues to spark the imaginations of people all over the world. Some believe that modern technology will eventually lead to the discovery of the wreck, while others think that the treasure is cursed and will never be found.

The story of the *Flor de la Mar* is a reminder of the risks and rewards of exploration during the Age of Discovery. In their quest for wealth and power, European explorers like Albuquerque faced great dangers, often venturing into uncharted waters and battling harsh conditions in search of fortune. While many succeeded in bringing back incredible riches, others, like the crew of the *Flor de la Mar*, paid the ultimate price for their ambition.

Even though the exact location of the *Flor de la Mar* and its treasure remains a mystery, the search for the lost gold continues to inspire new generations of adventurers. Whether the treasure is ever found or not, the legend of the *Flor de la Mar* will continue to be one of the most exciting and enduring stories of lost fortune in the history of the seas. Perhaps, one day, a daring explorer will uncover the wreck, and the lost gold of the *Flor de la Mar* will finally see the light of day again. Until then, the mystery of the *Flor de la Mar* remains one of the greatest unsolved treasures in history, hidden somewhere beneath the waves, waiting to be discovered.

Chapter 9: Pirate Ships of the Caribbean

The Caribbean Sea is famous for its turquoise waters, beautiful islands, and sandy beaches, but during the 17th and 18th centuries, it was also known as a dangerous place full of pirates and privateers. The Golden Age of Piracy, which lasted from about 1650 to 1730, was a time when daring and ruthless pirates ruled the seas, especially in the Caribbean. Pirate ships became legendary for their fast and stealthy attacks, where they would swoop in on unsuspecting merchant ships and plunder their treasures. These pirates used a variety of ships, but the most famous ones were swift, heavily armed, and perfectly suited for life at sea.

Pirates of the Caribbean were a mix of adventurers, escaped prisoners, sailors looking for fortune, and even some who had been forced into piracy. These pirates sailed the Caribbean for one main reason: treasure. During this time, European nations like Spain, England, France, and the Netherlands were expanding their colonies in the New World, and ships carrying gold, silver, spices, sugar, and other valuable goods sailed back and forth between Europe and the Americas. Pirates saw these ships as easy targets, and the Caribbean became one of the most dangerous places to sail.

Pirate ships in the Caribbean were chosen for their speed and maneuverability. The most famous pirate ship type was the sloop. Sloops were small, fast ships with a single mast and a large sail, making them perfect for quick getaways and surprise attacks. They could easily navigate the shallow waters and hidden coves of the Caribbean islands, which made it easier for pirates to hide from naval forces that tried to hunt them down. Sloops usually carried a crew of around 75 to 100 men, and they were armed with cannons and swivel guns, smaller guns that could be moved around the ship to fire at enemies during close combat.

Another popular pirate ship was the brigantine. Brigantines were slightly larger than sloops and had two masts, which gave them more speed and power. They could carry more cannons and a larger crew, which made them more dangerous in battle. Pirate captains liked brigantines because they could attack larger, slower merchant ships and still escape quickly if they were being pursued by naval ships. Some pirates even managed to capture large warships or merchant vessels and convert them into pirate ships by arming them with more cannons and fortifying the deck to prepare for battle.

Pirates chose their ships carefully, but the most important thing to them was how fast their ship could sail. They needed to be able to chase down heavily loaded merchant ships, which were often slow because of the weight of their cargo. Once the pirates caught up to their prey, they would use a combination of intimidation and force to take over the ship. Most pirate attacks didn't involve long, drawn-out battles. Pirates preferred to strike fast, firing a few cannon shots to scare their victims, and then boarding the ship to take control. Many merchant ships surrendered without a fight because they knew that resisting the pirates could lead to terrible consequences.

One of the most famous pirate ships of the Caribbean was *Queen Anne's Revenge*, the flagship of the notorious pirate Blackbeard. *Queen Anne's Revenge* was originally a French slave ship called *La Concorde*, but Blackbeard captured it in 1717 and transformed it into one of the most feared pirate ships of the time. He added more cannons to the ship, bringing the total number to 40, and used it to terrorize the waters off the coast of North America and the Caribbean. Blackbeard and his crew of over 300 men used *Queen Anne's Revenge* to blockade the port of Charleston, South Carolina, demanding medicine and supplies in exchange for the release of hostages. Blackbeard's reputation for being ruthless and intimidating was so strong that many ships would surrender to him without a fight.

Another famous pirate ship was *Whydah Galley*, which was commanded by the pirate Samuel "Black Sam" Bellamy. *Whydah* was originally a slave ship as well, but after Bellamy captured it, he turned it into a pirate ship, outfitting it with 28 cannons. Bellamy became known as the "Prince of Pirates" because he treated his captives with respect and fairness, unlike many other pirates. The *Whydah* became one of the most successful pirate ships in history, capturing dozens of ships in the Caribbean and along the American coast. Unfortunately, in 1717, *Whydah* sank in a storm off the coast of Cape Cod, Massachusetts, taking its treasure with it to the bottom of the sea. In the 1980s, the wreck of *Whydah* was discovered, and many artifacts and treasures from the ship have since been recovered.

The *Royal Fortune* was another pirate ship that made a name for itself in the Caribbean. It was the flagship of Bartholomew Roberts, also known as "Black Bart," who is considered one of the most successful pirates of all time. Black Bart captured hundreds of ships during his pirate career, and he used several different ships named *Royal Fortune* to carry out his raids. Roberts was known for being a skilled navigator and a daring captain who wasn't afraid to take on larger, more heavily armed ships. His *Royal Fortune* was a formidable ship, armed with dozens of cannons and manned by a large crew. Roberts operated not only in the Caribbean but also off the coast of West Africa, capturing valuable ships and goods.

Pirate ships were not just about battle and treasure hunting; they were also floating homes for the pirates who lived aboard them. Life on a pirate ship was rough and dangerous, but it was also filled with adventure and camaraderie. Pirate crews were often made up of men from all over the world, and the ships were surprisingly democratic. Most pirate ships followed a strict code of conduct, known as the "Pirate Code" or "Articles of Agreement." These rules were agreed upon by the entire crew and covered everything from how treasure was divided to how disputes between crew members were settled. On many pirate ships, the captain was elected by the crew, and while the captain had control during battles and raids, the crew had a say in most decisions.

One of the most important aspects of life on a pirate ship was the division of the loot. When a pirate crew captured a ship, the treasure was divided equally among the crew, with the captain and officers usually receiving a larger share. Injured crew members were often compensated with extra treasure to make up for the risks they had taken in battle. This system of sharing the wealth was one of the reasons many sailors were attracted to piracy; it offered them a chance to get rich quickly, especially compared to the hard and often poorly paid life of a sailor in the navy or on merchant ships.

The pirate ships of the Caribbean were also known for their colorful flags, the most famous of which was the Jolly Roger. The Jolly Roger was the pirate flag that typically featured a skull and crossbones, and it was flown to strike fear into the hearts of merchant ships. Each pirate captain had their own version of the Jolly Roger, and the flags often had symbols that represented death, danger, or defiance. Pirates would hoist the Jolly Roger just before attacking a ship, letting their enemies know that they were facing pirates. The sight of the Jolly Roger was often enough to make merchant ships surrender without a fight.

Pirate ships also had to be self-sufficient, as pirates often spent months at sea without returning to port. Pirates would stock their ships with food, water, and supplies before heading out on a voyage, but they also relied on capturing ships to resupply. They would take food, rum, and other necessities from captured ships, and they often raided coastal towns and settlements to get what they needed. Life aboard a pirate ship was tough; the conditions were cramped, food often ran low, and disease was common. Pirates also faced the constant threat of capture by naval forces, who were always on the lookout for pirate ships to hunt down.

Pirates of the Caribbean were constantly being pursued by the navies of the European powers, particularly the British, Spanish, and French. These countries sent warships to patrol the Caribbean and protect their merchant ships from pirate attacks. When a pirate ship was captured, the pirates were often put on trial and, if found guilty, hanged. Despite the dangers, many pirates continued their life of crime, drawn by the lure of treasure and the freedom of the open sea.

One of the most infamous pirate havens in the Caribbean was the island of Tortuga, located off the northern coast of Haiti. Tortuga became a stronghold for pirates, particularly the French buccaneers, who used the island as a base to launch raids against Spanish ships and settlements. The island was difficult for naval forces to control because of its rugged terrain and hidden harbors, making it an ideal refuge for pirates. Another famous pirate stronghold was Port Royal in Jamaica, which was known as the "wickedest city on earth" because of the number of pirates and criminals who lived there. Port Royal was a bustling port where pirates could sell their stolen goods, resupply their ships, and spend their loot on food, drink, and entertainment.

As the Golden Age of Piracy came to an end in the early 18th century, the Caribbean became safer for merchant ships, and the pirate ships that once roamed the seas gradually disappeared. The rise of powerful navies and the increased efforts by European governments to hunt down pirates made piracy less attractive and far more dangerous. Many pirates were captured and executed, while others accepted royal pardons in exchange for giving up their life of crime.

However, the legacy of the pirate ships of the Caribbean lives on. The stories of daring pirate captains, hidden treasure, and epic sea battles continue to captivate the imaginations of people today. Books, movies, and television shows about pirates, such as *Treasure Island* and *Pirates of the Caribbean*, have kept the legend of the pirate ships alive. These ships, with their black flags and dangerous crews, remain symbols of adventure, freedom, and the excitement of the open seas.

Even though the days of real-life pirate ships have long passed, the allure of the pirate life continues to inspire new generations of adventurers.

Chapter 10: The Disappearance of the USS Cyclops

The disappearance of the USS *Cyclops* is one of the greatest maritime mysteries in history, a tale filled with intrigue, unanswered questions, and a sense of wonder about how a massive ship could vanish without a trace. The USS *Cyclops* was a United States Navy ship that went missing in 1918 during World War I. Despite numerous searches and investigations, the ship was never found, and the cause of its disappearance remains unknown. Over the years, the story of the USS *Cyclops* has become one of the most famous cases associated with the Bermuda Triangle, a region in the Atlantic Ocean known for mysterious disappearances of ships and aircraft.

The USS *Cyclops* was a Proteus-class collier, which means it was a large cargo ship designed to carry coal for fueling naval vessels. It was one of the largest ships in the US Navy at the time, measuring 542 feet long and capable of carrying up to 12,500 tons of coal. The *Cyclops* was built to be strong and sturdy, with a steel hull and powerful engines that allowed it to travel across the ocean carrying heavy loads. It was commissioned in 1910 and played an important role in supplying coal to American and Allied warships during World War I.

In early 1918, the USS *Cyclops* was assigned a critical mission. The ship was to transport a large cargo of manganese ore, a heavy material used in the production of steel, from Brazil to the United States. The manganese was intended for use in making steel for the war effort, as World War I was still raging in Europe. On February 16, 1918, the *Cyclops* left the port of Rio de Janeiro, Brazil, with a crew of 309 men and a cargo of about 10,800 tons of manganese ore. The ship made a brief stop in Barbados on March 3 to resupply and make some minor repairs before setting off on the final leg of its journey to Baltimore, Maryland.

Everything seemed normal as the *Cyclops* left Barbados and sailed into the open Atlantic. The weather was calm, and there were no reports of any trouble from the ship. But as the days passed, the *Cyclops* failed to arrive at its destination. No distress signals were sent, and no one reported seeing the ship after it left Barbados. It was as if the *Cyclops* had simply vanished into thin air. When the ship was overdue, the US Navy launched an extensive search, covering thousands of square miles of the ocean in an attempt to locate the missing vessel. Ships and planes scoured the waters between the Caribbean and the East Coast of the United States, but there was no sign of the *Cyclops* or its crew. No wreckage, no lifeboats, and no bodies were ever found.

The disappearance of the USS *Cyclops* shocked the world. How could such a large and powerful ship vanish without leaving any clues? The mystery grew even deeper because the ship had not sent out any distress signals, which it should have been able to do if it were in trouble. The *Cyclops* was equipped with wireless radio communication, and it had plenty of lifeboats and safety equipment on board. Yet, there was no trace of the ship or its crew, and no one could explain what had happened.

Over the years, many theories have been proposed to explain the disappearance of the USS *Cyclops*. Some believe that the ship was sunk by a German U-boat, as the incident occurred during World War I, and German submarines were known to patrol the Atlantic at that time. However, there is no evidence to support this theory, as the Germans never claimed responsibility for sinking the *Cyclops*, and no records of a submarine attack in that area have ever been found.

Another theory suggests that the ship was lost due to a structural failure. The *Cyclops* was carrying an unusually heavy load of manganese ore, which may have made the ship unstable. Some experts believe that the weight of the cargo could have caused the ship to break apart during a storm or heavy seas. However, the weather at the time of the ship's disappearance was reported to be calm, and the ship was built to carry large loads, so it's unclear whether this was the cause.

One of the more mysterious theories involves the Bermuda Triangle, a region of the Atlantic Ocean bounded by Miami, Bermuda, and Puerto Rico, which has become famous for strange disappearances of ships and planes. The USS *Cyclops* was sailing through an area near the Bermuda Triangle when it disappeared, leading some to speculate that the ship fell victim to the mysterious forces that are said to cause ships and aircraft to vanish in the region. The Bermuda Triangle has long been associated with strange phenomena, such as magnetic anomalies, time warps, and even alien abductions, though these explanations are generally considered to be more myth than reality.

Another possibility is that the ship was sunk by a massive wave or freak weather event, such as a rogue wave or waterspout. Rogue waves are extremely large and powerful waves that can appear suddenly in the open ocean, and they have been known to sink ships without warning. Waterspouts, which are tornadoes that form over water, can also be dangerous to ships. However, there is no concrete evidence to suggest that such an event occurred at the time of the *Cyclops'* disappearance.

Some historians have suggested that sabotage or mutiny could have played a role in the ship's fate. The *Cyclops* had a diverse crew, including many men from different countries and backgrounds, and there were reports of unrest among the crew in the weeks leading up to the disappearance. The ship's captain, Lieutenant Commander George Worley, was also a controversial figure. Worley, who was born in Germany under the name Johan Frederick Wichmann, had a reputation for being a harsh and unpopular leader. Some have speculated that there may have been a mutiny on board the ship, or that Worley could have sabotaged the ship for personal reasons, possibly as an act of treachery during wartime. However, there is no solid evidence to support these claims.

Despite all these theories, the truth behind the disappearance of the USS *Cyclops* remains elusive. The ship's wreckage has never been found, and without any physical evidence, it is impossible to know for sure what happened. Over the years, other ships from the same class as the *Cyclops*, including the USS *Proteus* and the USS *Nereus*, also disappeared under mysterious circumstances in the Atlantic, leading some to wonder whether there was a design flaw in the ships that caused them to sink.

In the decades since the disappearance of the *Cyclops*, the ship has become a symbol of the enduring mysteries of the sea. The story has inspired countless books, documentaries, and television shows, and it continues to captivate people's imaginations. The idea that a massive ship could vanish without a trace, leaving behind no clues as to its fate, is both fascinating and unsettling. It reminds us of the power and unpredictability of the ocean, a vast and often unforgiving place where even the most advanced ships can be swallowed up without warning.

The disappearance of the USS *Cyclops* is also a reminder of the dangers faced by sailors during wartime. The men aboard the *Cyclops* were serving their country during a time of great conflict, and their loss was a tragedy for their families and for the Navy. Even though the exact cause of their disappearance may never be known, their story continues to be told as part of the history of the United States Navy.

In recent years, advances in technology have made it possible to search deeper and more thoroughly for shipwrecks in the ocean. Underwater robots, sonar, and other tools have helped researchers discover shipwrecks that were previously thought to be lost forever. Some believe that one day, the wreck of the USS *Cyclops* may be found, providing answers to the questions that have lingered for more than a century. If the ship is ever discovered, it could reveal valuable information about what caused its disappearance, whether it was a structural failure, an act of war, or something more mysterious.

Until then, the fate of the USS *Cyclops* remains one of the greatest unsolved mysteries of the sea. The ship and its crew have become part of maritime legend, joining the ranks of other famous lost ships like the *Mary Celeste* and the *Flying Dutchman*. The ocean is a place of wonder and mystery, and despite all our advances in technology and knowledge, there are still parts of the sea that remain unexplored and unknown. The disappearance of the USS *Cyclops* is a powerful reminder of the vastness of the ocean and the secrets it holds.

For the families of the men who were lost aboard the *Cyclops*, the mystery is a deeply personal one. They never received closure or a clear explanation of what happened to their loved ones. Over 300 men were lost when the ship vanished, and their memory lives on in the stories that have been passed down through generations. The Navy has never forgotten the loss of the *Cyclops*, and the ship is remembered as part of the history of World War I and the sacrifices made by those who served.

The mystery of the USS *Cyclops* will likely continue to captivate and intrigue people for years to come. Whether it was lost to a natural disaster, a human mistake, or something more supernatural, the story of the ship's disappearance is a reminder that, despite all we know, there are still many mysteries left to be solved in the world, especially in the deep, dark waters of the ocean.

Chapter 11: Treasures of the Deep Mediterranean

The Mediterranean Sea is one of the most ancient and historically rich bodies of water in the world. For thousands of years, it has been a central hub for trade, exploration, warfare, and the exchange of cultures between Europe, Asia, and Africa. Beneath its sparkling blue waters lie not only the remnants of great civilizations but also an incredible array of hidden treasures. These treasures, both real and legendary, tell stories of sunken ships, lost cities, and forgotten artifacts that have been buried in the deep for centuries. From the treasures of ancient empires to the wealth of pirates and lost merchant ships, the Mediterranean Sea is a mysterious vault filled with priceless secrets waiting to be discovered.

Throughout history, the Mediterranean has been a vital trade route for civilizations like the Egyptians, Phoenicians, Greeks, Romans, Byzantines, and many others. Ships loaded with goods like gold, silver, pottery, jewelry, spices, and textiles sailed these waters, often facing treacherous storms, attacks from pirates, or even the threat of war. Many of these ships never made it to their destinations and were lost beneath the waves, their cargoes sinking to the ocean floor where they have remained for centuries.

One of the most famous shipwrecks in the Mediterranean is that of the *Uluburun*, an ancient trading ship that sank off the coast of what is now Turkey around 1300 BCE. Discovered by a sponge diver in 1982, the wreck of the *Uluburun* has been described as one of the most important archaeological finds in history. The ship was carrying a massive cargo of luxury goods from all over the ancient world, including gold and silver jewelry, ivory, copper ingots, rare wood, and even glass beads. The artifacts recovered from the shipwreck offer a glimpse into the trade networks that existed during the Late Bronze Age and provide valuable information about the interactions between different cultures in the Mediterranean region. The treasures of the *Uluburun* shipwreck are now displayed in museums, but the sea still holds many other sunken vessels that have yet to be found.

The Roman Empire, which controlled much of the Mediterranean for centuries, was also responsible for many shipwrecks. Roman ships, known as triremes and merchant vessels, often carried valuable goods like wine, olive oil, grain, and luxury items across the sea. Some of these ships were lost during naval battles or due to natural disasters. One of the most significant Roman shipwreck discoveries was made off the coast of Italy near the island of Ventotene, where a group of five Roman ships was found. These ships, dating from the 1st century BCE to the 4th century CE, were carrying a variety of cargo, including large jars of wine and olive oil, lead ingots, and bronze artifacts. The discovery of these ships has provided archaeologists with a wealth of information about Roman trade routes and the types of goods that were transported across the Mediterranean.

One of the most exciting aspects of exploring the treasures of the Mediterranean is the discovery of ancient cities and settlements that have been submerged by the sea. The city of Heracleion, also known as Thonis, was an important port city in ancient Egypt that disappeared beneath the waters of the Mediterranean over a thousand years ago. For centuries, the city was believed to be a myth, but in 2000, a team of underwater archaeologists led by Franck Goddio discovered the remains of Heracleion off the coast of Egypt. The city had sunk due to a combination of rising sea levels, earthquakes, and subsidence of the land. Among the treasures found in Heracleion were giant statues of Egyptian gods, gold coins, intricate jewelry, and dozens of shipwrecks filled with goods. The discovery of Heracleion was a major archaeological breakthrough, and it showed that the Mediterranean still holds many secrets waiting to be uncovered.

Another famous submerged city is Pavlopetri, located off the coast of Greece. Pavlopetri is believed to be the oldest submerged city in the world, dating back over 5,000 years to the time of the Mycenaean civilization. The city was an important trading center during the Bronze Age and was likely abandoned after a series of earthquakes caused it to sink beneath the waves. Today, the ruins of Pavlopetri remain remarkably well-preserved, with streets, buildings, and even a cemetery visible beneath the water. Although no major treasures have been found at Pavlopetri, the city itself is a priceless archaeological treasure that offers insights into the lives of people who lived thousands of years ago.

In addition to ancient shipwrecks and lost cities, the Mediterranean has also been home to countless pirates and privateers who sailed its waters in search of treasure. Pirates have been a part of Mediterranean history for as long as people have been sailing these waters. The pirates of the Barbary Coast, based in what is now modern-day Tunisia, Algeria, and Morocco, were some of the most feared in the Mediterranean. These pirates, also known as corsairs, attacked ships from European countries, capturing cargo and taking prisoners to sell into slavery. Many of the treasures stolen by these pirates were hidden away in secret caches along the coast or buried on remote islands. While some pirate treasures have been found, many remain undiscovered, buried beneath the sands or hidden in underwater caves.

One of the most legendary pirate treasures of the Mediterranean is associated with the Knights of Malta, a group of Christian warrior-monks who defended the island of Malta from Muslim invaders during the Middle Ages. The Knights of Malta were known for their wealth, which they accumulated through donations, plunder, and piracy. According to legend, the knights hid a vast treasure somewhere on the island or in the waters surrounding it, and it has never been found. Treasure hunters have searched for centuries, but the location of the Knights of Malta's treasure remains a mystery.

In more modern times, the Mediterranean continued to be a site of naval conflict and treasure-laden shipwrecks. During both World Wars, the Mediterranean was the scene of intense naval battles, and many ships were sunk while carrying valuable cargoes. In World War II, German U-boats patrolled the Mediterranean, sinking Allied ships as they tried to transport supplies to troops in North Africa and Europe. One famous shipwreck from this period is that of the SS *President Coolidge*, an American luxury liner that was converted into a troopship during the war. The ship struck a mine off the coast of Egypt in 1942 and sank, taking with it a large amount of military equipment and supplies, including vehicles, weapons, and possibly even gold. While much of the wreck has been explored, there are still rumors that some of the treasure it was carrying remains hidden beneath the sea.

Another mysterious treasure story involves the shipwreck of the Spanish galleon *Nuestra Señora de las Mercedes*. In 1804, the *Mercedes* was part of a Spanish fleet carrying a massive fortune in gold and silver coins from the Americas to Spain. The ship was attacked and sunk by the British Navy near the coast of Portugal, and the treasure was lost to the depths of the sea. In 2007, a team of American treasure hunters working for a company called Odyssey Marine Exploration discovered the wreck and recovered over 500,000 silver and gold coins, worth an estimated $500 million. However, the Spanish government claimed ownership of the treasure, arguing that it belonged to Spain, and after a lengthy legal battle, the treasure was returned to Spain in 2012.

Despite modern technology and centuries of exploration, much of the Mediterranean remains unexplored, and many treasures are still waiting to be discovered. Advances in underwater archaeology and technology have made it easier to locate and explore shipwrecks and submerged sites. Remotely operated vehicles (ROVs), sonar mapping, and other tools allow researchers to search deeper and more thoroughly than ever before. These technologies have led to the discovery of previously unknown shipwrecks and artifacts that have been lost for thousands of years.

One of the challenges of recovering treasures from the deep Mediterranean is that many of the shipwrecks are located at extreme depths, sometimes more than a mile below the surface. These deep-water wrecks are often well-preserved because they are out of reach of looters, strong currents, and other forces that can damage or scatter artifacts. However, recovering treasure from these depths is extremely difficult and expensive, requiring specialized equipment and expertise.

Another challenge is the legal and ethical questions surrounding the recovery of underwater treasures. Many countries in the Mediterranean, such as Greece, Italy, and Turkey, have strict laws protecting shipwrecks and underwater archaeological sites. These countries view the artifacts and treasures as part of their cultural heritage, and they are concerned about the damage that treasure hunters can cause. In some cases, international treaties have been signed to protect underwater heritage and ensure that artifacts are preserved for future generations.

Despite these challenges, the allure of finding lost treasures in the Mediterranean continues to attract explorers and treasure hunters. The idea of discovering a sunken ship filled with gold coins, ancient jewelry, or priceless artifacts is a dream that has captivated people for centuries. The treasures of the deep Mediterranean represent not only immense wealth but also a connection to the past, a way to uncover the history of civilizations that have long since vanished.

Some of the treasures may never be found, hidden too deep or too well, but others may still be waiting, just beyond the reach of current technology. Every discovery made in the Mediterranean brings us closer to understanding the vast history that lies beneath the waves. Whether it's the remains of a Roman cargo ship, a pirate's stolen loot, or the sunken ruins of an ancient city, the treasures of the deep

Mediterranean are a testament to the enduring mysteries of the sea and the fascinating stories that still wait to be told.

Chapter 12: The Mystery of the Titanic's Sister Ship

The mystery of the Titanic's sister ship refers to the fascinating and often overlooked story of the RMS *Britannic*, one of three ships built as part of the White Star Line's Olympic-class vessels. These three ships—the *Olympic*, the *Titanic*, and the *Britannic*—were designed to be the largest and most luxurious ocean liners in the world. While the *Titanic's* tragic sinking in 1912 is widely known, the *Britannic's* story remains a lesser-known but equally intriguing chapter in maritime history. The *Britannic*, despite being the younger and supposedly safer sister ship of the *Titanic*, also met a tragic and mysterious end, raising many questions about its fate and what really happened during its final voyage.

The RMS *Britannic* was launched in 1914, two years after the sinking of the *Titanic*. At the time, White Star Line was eager to rebuild its reputation after the disaster of the *Titanic*, and the *Britannic* was intended to be an improved version of its ill-fated sister. Originally, the *Britannic* was designed to be a transatlantic passenger liner, just like the *Titanic*. It was meant to ferry wealthy passengers across the Atlantic, offering them the finest luxury and comfort available at sea. In fact, the *Britannic* was to be even more luxurious than the *Titanic*, with additional safety features designed to prevent another disaster like the one that had shocked the world just a few years earlier.

After the sinking of the *Titanic*, the designers of the *Britannic* made several important changes to ensure the new ship would be safer. One of the biggest improvements was in the lifeboat system. On the *Titanic*, there were not enough lifeboats for all of the passengers and crew, which was one of the main reasons why so many people lost their lives when the ship sank. For the *Britannic*, White Star Line added enough lifeboats for everyone on board, and they were distributed along the ship's deck in such a way that they could be easily launched, even if the ship was tilting.

In addition to the lifeboats, the *Britannic* was built with a stronger hull and more watertight compartments than the *Titanic*. The watertight compartments were designed to prevent water from flooding the entire ship in the event of a collision or damage to the hull. These improvements were meant to make the *Britannic* "unsinkable," much like the *Titanic* had been described before its tragic maiden voyage. Unfortunately, as history would later show, even these precautions were not enough to save the ship.

Despite all the safety improvements, the *Britannic* never got the chance to fulfill its role as a luxury passenger liner. Shortly after its completion, World War I broke out in Europe, and the British government requisitioned the ship to serve as a hospital vessel for the war effort. The *Britannic* was converted into a floating hospital and renamed His Majesty's Hospital Ship (HMHS) *Britannic*. Its grand halls and luxurious cabins were transformed into wards for wounded soldiers, and the ship was painted white with large red crosses on its sides to indicate that it was a hospital ship, which, under the rules of war, meant it should not be attacked.

The *Britannic* made several successful voyages between Britain and the Mediterranean, transporting injured soldiers from the front lines back to England for medical treatment. The ship was fast, spacious, and well-suited for its new role as a hospital ship. Everything seemed to be going smoothly, and the *Britannic* was performing its duties admirably. However, on November 21, 1916, the ship's fate took a tragic turn, just like its sister, the *Titanic*.

On that fateful morning, the *Britannic* was sailing through the Aegean Sea, near the island of Kea in Greece, when disaster struck. At approximately 8:12 a.m., there was a sudden and massive explosion near the front of the ship. The explosion caused significant damage to the hull, and water began pouring into the lower compartments.

Within minutes, it became clear that the ship was sinking. Despite the improvements made to the *Britannic* after the *Titanic* disaster, the ship's watertight compartments were not enough to stop the flooding, and the *Britannic* began to list to one side.

The exact cause of the explosion has been the subject of much debate and speculation over the years. Some historians believe that the *Britannic* struck a German naval mine, which had been planted in the waters as part of the war effort. Others suggest that the ship may have been torpedoed by a German U-boat, although no evidence of a torpedo attack has ever been found. The explosion's cause remains a mystery, adding an eerie layer of intrigue to the story of the *Britannic*'s sinking.

One of the factors that made the sinking of the *Britannic* so mysterious was how quickly the ship went down. Despite being larger and supposedly safer than the *Titanic*, the *Britannic* sank in less than an hour, much faster than the two and a half hours it took for the *Titanic* to disappear beneath the waves. The speed at which the *Britannic* sank was alarming, and it left little time for the crew and medical staff to organize an orderly evacuation.

As the water continued to flood the lower decks, the captain of the *Britannic*, Charles Bartlett, made the decision to beach the ship on the nearby island of Kea in an attempt to prevent it from sinking. He ordered full speed ahead in the hopes of running the ship aground, where it could be evacuated safely. Unfortunately, the increasing list of the ship and the flooding of the engine room made this impossible. The ship was sinking too quickly, and it was clear that it would not reach the shore in time.

The crew and medical staff quickly began lowering lifeboats into the water. The evacuation was more organized than that of the *Titanic*, thanks in part to the increased number of lifeboats and the experience gained from the previous disaster. However, the sinking of the *Britannic* was not without its own tragic moments. Some of the lifeboats were launched too early, and they were caught in the ship's still-turning propellers. As the massive blades continued to churn through the water, they destroyed several of the lifeboats, killing dozens of people in the process. It was a horrific scene, and the loss of life was devastating.

Despite the chaos, many people were able to escape the sinking ship. Of the 1,065 people on board, 1,035 survived, a far better outcome than the *Titanic*'s disaster. The relatively low number of casualties was due in large part to the fact that the *Britannic* was sailing in warm, calm waters, and there were rescue ships nearby that could assist in the evacuation. The survivors were taken to nearby islands and later rescued by British ships.

The sinking of the *Britannic* left behind many unanswered questions. Why did the ship sink so quickly? What caused the explosion in the first place? Why did the improved safety features fail to prevent the disaster? These questions have intrigued historians, maritime experts, and shipwreck enthusiasts for decades. Some believe that the ship's watertight compartments were compromised by the explosion, allowing water to flood into areas that should have been sealed off. Others suggest that the open portholes on the lower decks, which were opened to provide ventilation for the wounded soldiers, allowed water to pour in at an accelerated rate.

In the years following the sinking, numerous attempts were made to locate the wreck of the *Britannic* and solve the mystery of what happened that day. In 1975, famous ocean explorer Jacques Cousteau and his team finally located the wreck of the *Britannic* in the Aegean Sea, lying on its side at a depth of about 400 feet. Cousteau's exploration of the wreck revealed that the ship had indeed been damaged by an external explosion, likely caused by a naval mine. However, the exact location of the mine and how it caused the ship to sink so rapidly remains a mystery.

The wreck of the *Britannic* is now a popular destination for divers and underwater archaeologists, and it is one of the largest and most intact shipwrecks in the world. Unlike the *Titanic*, which lies at a much greater depth in the Atlantic Ocean, the *Britannic* is more accessible to divers, and many expeditions have been made to explore its remains. The wreck has provided valuable insights into the design of the ship and the circumstances of its sinking, but many mysteries still surround the *Britannic*'s final moments.

The *Britannic* was the last of the Olympic-class ships to be lost at sea, marking the end of an era for White Star Line. Its sister ship, the *Olympic*, continued to serve as a passenger liner and troopship during World War I, earning the nickname "Old Reliable" for its many successful voyages. The *Olympic* was eventually retired in the 1930s and scrapped, leaving the *Britannic* as the final mystery in the saga of the Titanic's sister ships.

Although the *Britannic*'s sinking did not result in the same loss of life or global shock as the *Titanic*, it remains a poignant and fascinating story. The ship's connection to the *Titanic* and its tragic end have kept its memory alive, and the ongoing mystery of what caused the explosion continues to captivate historians and maritime enthusiasts alike. Today, the *Britannic* lies peacefully on the ocean floor, a silent testament to the dangers of the sea and the enduring mysteries of the ocean's greatest ships.

Chapter 13: The Sunken Silver of the San José

The story of the sunken silver of the *San José* is one of the most legendary and mysterious tales of treasure lost at sea. It's a story that combines history, adventure, naval warfare, and an incredible fortune of gold, silver, and precious gems, all lying at the bottom of the ocean for over 300 years. The *San José* was a Spanish galleon, a massive and heavily armed ship built to transport valuable cargoes across the Atlantic from the Spanish colonies in the Americas to Spain. On its final voyage in 1708, the *San José* carried one of the richest treasures ever assembled—treasure that has never been recovered and remains lost beneath the waves.

The tale begins during the early 18th century, a time when Spain was one of the most powerful empires in the world. The Spanish had vast colonies in South and Central America, places like modern-day Colombia, Peru, and Mexico, where they mined huge quantities of silver, gold, and other precious materials. Every year, Spain would send large fleets of ships, known as treasure fleets, to transport these riches back to Europe. These fleets would sail across the Atlantic, laden with silver coins, gold bars, and valuable goods like emeralds, pearls, and spices. The treasure fleets were vital to the Spanish economy, providing the funds that kept the Spanish Empire running and enabling the country to pay for its wars, its armies, and its grand palaces.

The *San José* was part of one of these treasure fleets, known as the *Galeón de Tierra Firme*, which sailed from the port of Cartagena in present-day Colombia. The ship was loaded with an enormous treasure, including more than 200 tons of silver coins, gold ingots, emeralds, and other valuables, all collected from the Spanish colonies in the Americas. The treasure on board the *San José* was destined for King Philip V of Spain, who needed the money to fund his efforts in the War of Spanish Succession, a conflict that had been raging in Europe since 1701.

The War of Spanish Succession was a major European conflict that pitted Spain and France against a coalition of countries that included Britain, the Netherlands, and Austria. At the heart of the war was a struggle over who would inherit the Spanish throne after the death of the last Spanish Habsburg king. The war was fought both on land and at sea, and naval power played a crucial role in the outcome. The British Royal Navy, in particular, was determined to disrupt Spain's treasure fleets and prevent the vast wealth of the Americas from reaching the Spanish king's coffers.

In June 1708, the *San José* set sail from Cartagena, accompanied by several other ships in the treasure fleet. The fleet was heavily armed and well-protected, as the Spanish knew that the waters of the Caribbean and the Atlantic were dangerous, filled with pirates, privateers, and enemy warships. The *San José* itself was one of the most powerful galleons in the fleet, equipped with 64 cannons and carrying hundreds of crew members and soldiers to defend the treasure. However, the Spanish were not the only ones aware of the immense riches being transported across the sea.

The British, having intercepted intelligence about the treasure fleet, sent a squadron of warships under the command of Admiral Charles Wager to intercept the *San José* and its companions. Admiral Wager's mission was clear: capture the treasure fleet, seize its valuable cargo, and deliver a devastating blow to Spain's war effort. On June 8, 1708, just off the coast of Cartagena near the Baru Peninsula in modern-day Colombia, the British warships caught up with the Spanish fleet. A fierce battle ensued, one that would decide the fate of one of the greatest treasures ever lost at sea.

The Battle of Baru, as it came to be known, was a brutal and chaotic fight. The British ships attacked the *San José* and its escorts, trying to board the galleons and capture their cargo. The Spanish, for their part, fought back fiercely, determined to protect their treasure and prevent it from falling into British hands. The *San José* was heavily outnumbered and outgunned, but its captain, José Fernández de Santillán, refused to surrender. As the battle raged on, disaster struck the *San José*.

At some point during the battle, the powder magazine of the *San José*—the area of the ship where gunpowder was stored for the cannons—was hit by enemy fire, causing a massive explosion. The explosion was so powerful that it tore the ship apart, sending it to the bottom of the sea in a matter of minutes. The treasure-laden galleon sank with all hands on board, taking with it the 200 tons of silver, gold, and precious gems that it had been carrying. Of the more than 600 crew members and soldiers on the ship, only a handful survived the explosion and were rescued by the British. The rest of the treasure fleet managed to escape, but the *San José*, along with its immense fortune, was lost forever in the depths of the Caribbean Sea.

For centuries, the location of the *San José* wreck remained a mystery. The ship had gone down quickly, and there were few clues as to where exactly it had sunk. Over the years, many treasure hunters, explorers, and governments tried to find the wreck, hoping to recover the vast fortune that had been lost. The estimated value of the treasure on board the *San José* has been a subject of much speculation, but modern estimates suggest that it could be worth as much as $17 billion today, making it one of the most valuable shipwrecks in history.

The search for the *San José* became something of a legend in the world of maritime archaeology and treasure hunting. Various expeditions were launched over the years to locate the wreck, but none were successful. The waters off the coast of Colombia are treacherous, with strong currents, deep trenches, and a seabed littered with the remains of other ships lost over the centuries. For a long time, it seemed as though the *San José* and its treasure would remain lost to history, hidden somewhere in the dark depths of the ocean.

However, in 2015, after more than 300 years of mystery, the wreck of the *San José* was finally discovered by a team of Colombian naval archaeologists and international researchers. Using state-of-the-art underwater technology, including sonar and remotely operated vehicles (ROVs), the team was able to locate the wreck at a depth of more than 2,000 feet. The discovery was a major breakthrough and caused a sensation around the world. Images from the underwater exploration showed the remains of the *San José* lying on the seabed, its cannons and other artifacts still remarkably well-preserved after centuries underwater.

The discovery of the *San José* reignited interest in the treasure that it had carried. The question of who owns the treasure became a major legal and political issue. The wreck lies in Colombian waters, and under international law, Colombia has the right to claim the wreck and any treasure it contains. However, Spain also staked a claim, arguing that the *San José* was a Spanish ship and that the treasure rightfully belongs to the Spanish crown. Additionally, descendants of the crew members who perished in the sinking have also made claims to the treasure, adding further complexity to the debate.

The Colombian government has declared the wreck of the *San José* to be a national treasure and has vowed to protect it from looters and treasure hunters. The site is now closely guarded, and any attempts to recover the treasure will be carefully monitored to ensure that the shipwreck and its artifacts are preserved for future generations. The Colombian government has also expressed its intention to create a museum dedicated to the *San José*, where the recovered artifacts and treasure could be displayed to the public.

Despite the discovery of the wreck, much of the *San José*'s treasure still lies on the ocean floor. Recovering the treasure from such great depths is a complex and expensive task that requires advanced technology and careful planning. The treasure is believed to be scattered across the seabed, mixed with the remains of the ship, its cannons, and other artifacts. While some of the treasure may eventually be recovered, much of it may remain lost forever, buried beneath layers of sediment and debris.

The mystery of the *San José* and its sunken silver continues to captivate people around the world. The ship's tragic sinking, the vast fortune it carried, and the intrigue surrounding its discovery have made it one of the most famous shipwrecks in history. For treasure hunters, historians, and adventurers alike, the *San José* represents the ultimate prize—a treasure lost for centuries, waiting to be uncovered.

The story of the *San José* is also a reminder of the dangers of naval warfare and the high stakes involved in the transportation of treasure during the age of exploration and empire. The Spanish treasure fleets, which brought immense wealth to Europe, also carried with them the risks of piracy, storms, and enemy attacks. Many ships like the *San José* never made it to their destinations, their treasures lost to the sea, and their stories left to the imagination of future generations.

In the years to come, as new technologies continue to improve, there may be further attempts to recover more of the treasure from the *San José* wreck. But even if the silver, gold, and emeralds are never fully recovered, the *San José* will remain a symbol of the enduring mysteries of the sea and the incredible fortunes that still lie hidden beneath the waves. The discovery of the shipwreck was a major achievement in the world of underwater archaeology, but it also raised as many questions as it answered. How much of the treasure remains intact? What artifacts and clues to the past will be uncovered in future explorations? And will the debate over the ownership of the treasure ever be fully resolved?

The *San José* and its lost treasure have become part of maritime lore, a tale that will continue to inspire curiosity and wonder for generations to come. Whether or not the sunken silver of the *San José* is ever fully recovered, the story of the galleon's final voyage and its place in history will never be forgotten.

Chapter 14: Lost Ships of the Ancient Romans

The Lost Ships of the Ancient Romans are one of the most fascinating mysteries of history, as they represent not only the incredible naval power of the Roman Empire but also the forgotten treasures, artifacts, and knowledge that might still lie hidden beneath the waves. The Romans were master sailors and traders who ruled much of the Mediterranean Sea for centuries, building a vast network of trade routes, military fleets, and ports. Their ships sailed all the way from the coasts of Britain in the north to the far reaches of Egypt and North Africa in the south, and from Spain in the west to the Middle East in the east. Over the centuries, thousands of Roman ships were lost at sea due to storms, naval battles, piracy, or simply the ravages of time. These lost ships represent an untold wealth of historical treasures, from gold coins and luxurious goods to military equipment and ancient knowledge, and the search for them continues to this day.

The Romans were among the greatest seafaring people of the ancient world. Their empire, which lasted for nearly a thousand years, stretched across three continents, and their navy played a crucial role in maintaining control over these vast territories. Roman ships were used for a variety of purposes, from transporting goods and raw materials to ferrying soldiers and war equipment. Roman merchant ships, known as *navis oneraria*, carried cargoes of grain, olive oil, wine, and other valuable commodities across the Mediterranean, while their warships, such as the famous *trireme* and *quadrireme*, were equipped with rows of oars and manned by highly trained crews of sailors and soldiers. These ships allowed the Romans to dominate the seas and ensure the smooth functioning of their empire.

However, the seas were dangerous, even for the Romans. Storms were a constant threat, especially in the open waters of the

Mediterranean, where sudden gales and powerful waves could sink even the sturdiest of ships. Piracy was also a serious problem, and Roman merchant ships were often targeted by pirates from places like the Greek islands or the coast of North Africa. Naval battles were another source of shipwrecks, as the Romans fought wars with rival powers such as Carthage, Greece, and later the Germanic tribes and other groups that sought to challenge Roman dominance. In addition to these dangers, there were natural hazards, like hidden reefs and rocky shorelines, that could tear a ship apart in moments. Over the centuries, countless Roman ships were lost, their remains sinking to the bottom of the sea along with their cargoes and crew.

One of the most famous lost Roman ships is the *Nemi Ships*, a pair of enormous ceremonial ships that were discovered at the bottom of Lake Nemi, near Rome. These ships were built during the reign of the Roman Emperor Caligula in the first century AD and were thought to be luxurious floating palaces used for religious ceremonies or imperial parties. The *Nemi Ships* were far larger than most other Roman ships, with ornate designs and luxurious accommodations, including marble floors, heated baths, and intricate mosaics. For centuries, these ships remained at the bottom of the lake, shrouded in mystery, until they were rediscovered in the early 20th century. Although much of the ships' contents were looted or damaged over the years, the discovery of the *Nemi Ships* provided valuable insight into Roman engineering and the grandeur of imperial Rome.

Another famous discovery was made off the coast of the Greek island of Antikythera in 1900, where a Roman shipwreck dating back to the first century BC was found by sponge divers. This ship, known as the *Antikythera wreck*, carried an astonishing cargo of treasures, including statues, pottery, and an extraordinary ancient device known as the *Antikythera Mechanism*. This mechanism, often described as the world's first analog computer, was a complex system of gears used to track the movements of the stars and planets. The discovery of the

Antikythera Mechanism stunned archaeologists and historians, as it showed a level of technological sophistication far beyond what was previously thought possible in the ancient world. This shipwreck also demonstrated the variety of valuable goods that Roman ships transported across the Mediterranean, from art and luxury goods to scientific instruments.

In addition to treasures and artifacts, lost Roman ships also tell the story of the vast Roman trade network that connected the different parts of the empire. Roman merchant ships regularly transported grain from Egypt, olive oil from Spain, wine from Italy, and pottery from North Africa to ports all over the Mediterranean. The remains of these ships, along with their cargoes, offer a glimpse into the daily life of the Roman Empire and the goods that were essential to its economy. Some Roman ships even ventured beyond the Mediterranean, trading with distant lands such as India, Arabia, and possibly even China. These long-distance voyages brought exotic goods like spices, silk, and precious stones to Roman markets, further enriching the empire and creating a thriving international trade network.

One of the most remarkable discoveries of a Roman shipwreck came in 1982, when a ship was found off the coast of Sicily, near the town of Gela. This ship, known as the *Gela wreck*, dates back to the fifth century BC, during the height of the Roman Republic. The ship was a merchant vessel, likely carrying goods between Italy and the Greek colonies in Sicily, and its discovery provided important insights into the early period of Roman naval trade. The cargo of the *Gela wreck* included amphorae, which were used to transport wine and oil, as well as pottery and other everyday items. The ship's well-preserved state allowed archaeologists to study its construction techniques and learn more about how the Romans built their ships during this period.

Roman naval warfare also left behind many lost ships, especially from the period of the Punic Wars, when Rome fought against the powerful maritime empire of Carthage. The Romans and

Carthaginians clashed in a series of naval battles as they fought for control of the Mediterranean, and many ships were lost during these encounters. The *Battle of the Aegates Islands* in 241 BC, for example, was a decisive naval battle that marked the end of the First Punic War. In this battle, the Roman fleet defeated the Carthaginians, sinking many of their ships and forcing them to surrender. Archaeologists have discovered the remains of several Carthaginian and Roman warships from this battle, including bronze rams, which were used to smash into enemy ships during combat. These discoveries provide valuable information about Roman naval tactics and the role of ships in warfare.

In the waters off the coast of Israel, archaeologists have found the remains of several Roman ships that sank while transporting goods between the Roman provinces in the eastern Mediterranean. These ships carried everything from food and supplies for Roman soldiers to luxury items like glassware and jewelry. One notable shipwreck, discovered near the ancient port of Caesarea, contained a treasure trove of Roman coins, gold rings, and bronze statues, all of which had been preserved by the sands of the sea for nearly 2,000 years. This shipwreck is a reminder of the immense wealth and trade that flowed through the Roman Empire, and the risks that sailors faced as they carried goods across the seas.

One of the most intriguing aspects of the lost ships of the Romans is the possibility that many more remain undiscovered beneath the sea. The Mediterranean is often referred to as a "graveyard of ships," as it has been sailed by countless vessels over thousands of years, and many of these ships have never been found. Advances in underwater archaeology, including sonar technology and remotely operated vehicles (ROVs), have made it possible to explore deeper and more inaccessible areas of the sea, leading to new discoveries of ancient shipwrecks. Some experts believe that there are still vast treasures, artifacts, and historical records waiting to be found, hidden among the lost ships of the Roman Empire.

One area that holds particular promise for future discoveries is the waters around the island of Sicily, which was a major hub of Roman trade and naval activity. Several important Roman shipwrecks have already been found in this region, and archaeologists believe that many more may be waiting to be discovered. The same is true for the coasts of Egypt, where Roman ships carried grain and other goods from the fertile lands of the Nile to feed the growing population of Rome. In addition to the potential for discovering valuable cargoes, these shipwrecks may also contain clues to the everyday lives of Roman sailors, traders, and soldiers, offering a unique glimpse into the world of ancient Rome.

The lost ships of the Romans continue to capture the imagination of historians, archaeologists, and treasure hunters alike. These ships represent not only the wealth and power of the Roman Empire but also the dangers and challenges faced by those who sailed its seas. Each new discovery adds to our understanding of Roman naval history and the role that ships played in shaping the empire. Whether they were carrying soldiers to distant battles, transporting luxury goods across the Mediterranean, or sinking in the midst of a fierce storm, the lost ships of the Romans hold the secrets of a world long gone, waiting to be uncovered and studied.

As we continue to explore the depths of the ocean, we are likely to uncover more lost ships from the Roman period, each one offering new insights into the ancient world. The treasures they carry, both literal and historical, remind us of the incredible reach and influence of the Roman Empire and the enduring mysteries that still lie beneath the waves. Whether it's the discovery of a new shipwreck or the excavation of an ancient cargo, the search for the lost ships of the Romans is an ongoing journey, one that promises to reveal more about the history of one of the greatest civilizations the world has ever known.

Chapter 15: The Enigma of the Japanese Submarine I-52

The enigma of the Japanese submarine *I-52* is one of the most intriguing mysteries of World War II. The *I-52* was a large, highly advanced submarine designed by the Imperial Japanese Navy, and it embarked on a secret mission in 1944 that would link two powerful Axis forces: Japan and Nazi Germany. What makes the story of the *I-52* so fascinating isn't just its advanced technology or the mission it was undertaking, but the fact that it sank to the bottom of the Atlantic Ocean, taking with it a secret cargo that has captured the imaginations of historians, treasure hunters, and adventurers ever since.

The *I-52* was part of a special type of Japanese submarines known as "submarine cruisers"—large, long-range vessels built for extended operations far from Japan. These submarines were capable of traveling great distances without needing to refuel or resupply, and they were among the most advanced in the world at the time. The *I-52*, in particular, was 356 feet long and displaced more than 2,500 tons, making it one of the largest submarines in the Japanese fleet. It was heavily armed with torpedoes, anti-aircraft guns, and even carried a small plane for reconnaissance missions. But what really made the *I-52* unique was its mission.

By 1944, the tide of World War II had turned against both Japan and Germany. Japan had suffered major defeats in the Pacific, losing key islands and naval battles to the United States, while Germany was struggling against the Allies in Europe. Despite their struggles, Japan and Germany were determined to support each other, and one of the ways they did this was by sending submarines on secret missions to exchange materials, technology, and intelligence. These missions, known as "Yanagi missions," involved Japanese submarines making the long and dangerous journey to German-controlled ports in Europe, carrying valuable cargo that would help both nations in their war efforts.

The *I-52* was assigned to one such mission. Its task was to travel from Japan to the French port of Lorient, which was then occupied by Germany, and deliver a secret cargo of raw materials that were desperately needed by the Nazis. In return, the submarine would receive advanced German technology, including radar systems, jet engine parts, and possibly even blueprints for new weapons. This mission was vital for both Japan and Germany, as the Axis powers were running low on key resources and technological innovations that could help them fight the Allies. The *I-52* set out from Kure, Japan, on March 10, 1944, carrying a cargo that included 146 tons of tin, tungsten, molybdenum, and rubber—valuable raw materials for the German war machine.

But that wasn't all the *I-52* carried. According to some reports, the submarine also had a secret cargo of gold bars, worth millions of dollars, meant to help finance the German war effort. The exact amount of gold on board has been the subject of much speculation, but it is believed to have been between two and five tons, making it one of the largest shipments of gold ever sent during the war. In addition to the cargo, the *I-52* carried a crew of 95 men, including sailors, engineers, and technicians who were trained to operate the submarine's complex systems. The submarine also had a few German passengers on board—specialists who were meant to help the Japanese install the advanced technology they would receive in Europe.

The *I-52* began its journey across the Pacific, heading south toward the Indian Ocean to avoid Allied naval patrols. After stopping briefly at Singapore to refuel and resupply, the submarine made its way through the Indian Ocean, passing through the dangerous waters that were patrolled by British and American ships. Despite the risks, the *I-52* managed to evade detection and continued its journey toward the Atlantic Ocean. The crew must have known how dangerous the mission was—by 1944, the Allies had gained control of much of the Atlantic, and German U-boats were being hunted by Allied aircraft and warships. Nevertheless, the *I-52* pressed on, determined to complete its mission.

To help the *I-52* avoid detection, the Germans sent a U-boat, the *U-530*, to rendezvous with the Japanese submarine in the middle of the Atlantic. The two submarines were supposed to meet and exchange information, allowing the Germans to guide the *I-52* safely to Lorient. But before this rendezvous could take place, the Allies received crucial intelligence that would change the course of the mission. American codebreakers, working in conjunction with British intelligence, had cracked the Japanese naval codes and learned about the *I-52*'s mission. Armed with this information, the U.S. Navy launched a top-secret operation to intercept and destroy the submarine before it could reach Europe.

The Americans deployed a specially equipped aircraft carrier, the USS *Bogue*, to search for the *I-52*. The *Bogue* carried a squadron of Grumman TBF Avenger torpedo bombers, which were equipped with advanced radar and sonar systems designed to locate and attack submarines. On the night of June 23, 1944, after several days of searching, the Avengers from the *Bogue* detected a radar contact in the middle of the Atlantic, about 850 miles west of the Cape Verde Islands. The contact turned out to be the *I-52*, which was cruising on the surface, unaware that it had been discovered.

The American bombers launched an immediate attack, dropping depth charges and acoustic torpedoes aimed at the submarine. The crew of the *I-52* tried to dive and escape, but it was too late. One of the torpedoes struck the submarine, causing a massive explosion. The *I-52* sank quickly, plunging to the bottom of the ocean with all hands on board. The American aircraft circled the area, dropping flares to mark the location of the wreck, and then returned to the *Bogue* to report their success. The *I-52* had been destroyed, along with its valuable cargo, and its mission was a failure.

For decades, the location of the *I-52*'s wreck remained a mystery. The submarine had sunk in the deep waters of the Atlantic, far from any major shipping lanes, and its exact coordinates were not widely known. But in the early 1990s, a marine treasure hunter named Paul Tidwell became interested in the story of the *I-52*. Tidwell had spent years searching for shipwrecks and lost treasure, and he believed that the *I-52* might hold a fortune in gold, as well as valuable historical artifacts from World War II. Tidwell began a meticulous search, using historical records, naval archives, and modern technology to pinpoint the location of the wreck.

In 1995, after years of searching, Tidwell's team located the wreck of the *I-52* more than 17,000 feet below the surface of the Atlantic Ocean. The wreck was found using sonar and remotely operated vehicles (ROVs), which sent back images of the submarine lying on the ocean floor, remarkably well-preserved despite its long time underwater. The discovery of the *I-52* was a major achievement, and it attracted international attention from historians, archaeologists, and treasure hunters.

However, the mystery of the *I-52* was far from over. Despite extensive exploration of the wreck, no gold has ever been found. Some experts believe that the gold may have been stored in a secret compartment on the submarine that has yet to be discovered, while others think that the gold may have been removed before the submarine embarked on its final mission. There are even theories that the *I-52* was carrying other secret cargo, such as valuable documents, weapons technology, or even uranium, which the Germans were working to develop into a nuclear bomb. These theories have fueled speculation and debate about the true purpose of the *I-52*'s mission and what secrets it may still hold.

In addition to the question of the gold, there is also the mystery of the submarine's crew. The *I-52* was carrying 95 men, all of whom perished when the submarine sank. Their remains are still entombed in the wreck, and there has been some discussion about whether the wreck should be left undisturbed as a war grave or whether further exploration should be allowed. The Japanese government has expressed interest in the site, and there have been efforts to honor the memory of the crew members who died in the sinking.

The wreck of the *I-52* remains one of the deepest shipwrecks ever found, and exploring it poses significant technical challenges. The extreme depth and pressure make it difficult to retrieve artifacts or conduct detailed surveys of the wreck, and there is always the risk of damaging the submarine or disturbing its contents. Despite these challenges, the search for answers continues, and new technologies may one day allow for a more thorough exploration of the wreck and the recovery of its long-lost treasures.

The story of the *I-52* is a reminder of the hidden dangers and mysteries of the sea, as well as the incredible feats of engineering and bravery that defined naval warfare during World War II. The submarine was a marvel of technology, capable of traveling thousands of miles across the ocean while carrying a secret cargo that could have changed the course of the war. Its mission, though ultimately unsuccessful, stands as a testament to the determination and ingenuity of both the Japanese and German militaries during the final years of the conflict.

Today, the wreck of the *I-52* lies in the dark, cold depths of the Atlantic Ocean, a silent witness to the deadly game of cat and mouse that played out on the world's oceans during World War II. Whether or not the submarine's gold and other secrets are ever fully uncovered, the enigma of the *I-52* will continue to fascinate and inspire those who seek to unravel the mysteries of the past.

Chapter 16: The Hidden Gold of the Merchant Royal

The story of the *Merchant Royal* is one of the most legendary tales of lost treasure at sea, filled with mystery, adventure, and the allure of unimaginable wealth hidden beneath the waves. Known as the "El Dorado of the Seas," the *Merchant Royal* was an English merchant ship that sank in 1641, taking with it one of the largest treasures ever lost in maritime history. The search for the ship and its lost gold has captivated treasure hunters and historians for centuries, and despite countless efforts to locate the wreck, the *Merchant Royal* and its treasure remain elusive, shrouded in mystery and speculation.

The *Merchant Royal* was a large and sturdy ship, built for long voyages across the Atlantic and the Mediterranean. It was captained by John Limbrey, an experienced seaman who had been in command of the vessel for several years. The ship was engaged in trade between England, Spain, and the New World, transporting goods such as spices, textiles, and precious metals. During its final voyage, the *Merchant Royal* was returning to England from the Spanish colonies in the Americas, carrying an extraordinary cargo of treasure, which included gold, silver, and valuable jewels. It is believed that the ship was transporting a fortune in Spanish treasure that had been collected as taxes and payments from the colonies and was being sent back to Europe to support the Spanish crown, which was heavily in debt at the time.

The exact amount of treasure aboard the *Merchant Royal* has been the subject of much debate and speculation. According to historical records, the ship was carrying an estimated 100,000 pounds of gold, 400 bars of silver, and 500,000 pieces of eight (Spanish silver coins), as well as a large quantity of other valuable goods. In today's terms, this treasure would be worth hundreds of millions, if not billions, of dollars.

It was one of the richest cargoes ever assembled, and its loss would become one of the greatest maritime disasters of the 17th century.

In September 1641, the *Merchant Royal* found itself off the coast of Cornwall, England, having completed most of its long voyage from the New World. The ship was heavily laden with treasure, and its crew had weathered storms and rough seas along the way. However, disaster struck when the ship began to leak, and despite the crew's best efforts to keep it afloat, the situation quickly worsened. The ship's pumps failed, and water began to flood the cargo holds. Captain Limbrey and his crew knew that the ship was doomed, and they made the decision to abandon the *Merchant Royal*.

As the ship sank beneath the waves, Captain Limbrey and some of his crew managed to escape in lifeboats, but many of the men aboard the ship were not so fortunate. It is said that 18 crew members went down with the ship, lost to the cold, rough seas. The survivors were eventually rescued by another ship, the *Dover Merchant*, which had been sailing nearby. But the *Merchant Royal* itself, along with its vast fortune, disappeared beneath the waves and was never seen again.

The sinking of the *Merchant Royal* sent shockwaves through Europe, particularly in England and Spain. The treasure aboard the ship was intended to help fund the Spanish government, which was struggling with economic problems and wars. Its loss was a major blow to the Spanish crown, and both the English and Spanish governments were desperate to recover the sunken treasure. However, locating a shipwreck in the open ocean in the 17th century was nearly impossible. The technology of the time was primitive, and there were no accurate charts or instruments to pinpoint the exact location where the ship had gone down. The *Merchant Royal* had sunk somewhere off the coast of Cornwall, but beyond that, the details were vague and uncertain.

Over the centuries, the *Merchant Royal* became the subject of countless legends and tales of hidden treasure. The idea of a shipwreck carrying a fortune in gold and silver lying at the bottom of the sea inspired adventurers, treasure hunters, and explorers to search for the wreck. Many have tried to find it, but the treacherous waters off the coast of Cornwall, with their strong currents, rocky seabed, and unpredictable weather, have made the search incredibly difficult. Despite modern technology and advancements in underwater exploration, the wreck of the *Merchant Royal* has never been conclusively found.

One of the main reasons the wreck has remained so elusive is the lack of precise information about where the ship actually sank. Captain Limbrey's accounts of the sinking are incomplete, and there are no reliable records that pinpoint the exact location. Some historians believe the ship went down in the deep waters off the Isles of Scilly, a group of islands off the southwestern tip of England, while others think it may be closer to the Cornish coast. The area where the ship is believed to have sunk is vast and difficult to search, even with modern equipment like sonar and remotely operated vehicles (ROVs).

In recent years, advances in marine technology have renewed interest in the search for the *Merchant Royal*. The development of deep-sea exploration equipment, such as submersibles and underwater drones, has made it possible to search previously inaccessible areas of the ocean floor. In addition, the use of sophisticated sonar and magnetometers, which can detect metal objects buried beneath the seabed, has given treasure hunters new tools to locate shipwrecks. Despite these advances, however, the *Merchant Royal* continues to remain hidden, and its exact location remains a mystery.

One of the most exciting moments in the search for the *Merchant Royal* came in 2007 when a team of treasure hunters working for the American salvage company Odyssey Marine Exploration discovered a shipwreck off the coast of Cornwall. The wreck was found in deep water, and initial reports suggested that it could be the long-lost *Merchant Royal*. The wreck contained a large amount of silver coins and other artifacts, and for a brief time, there was speculation that the treasure of the *Merchant Royal* had finally been found. However, further analysis revealed that the wreck was not the *Merchant Royal*, but another ship of similar age and size.

The discovery of this wreck only fueled further interest in the *Merchant Royal*, as it showed that there were still valuable shipwrecks waiting to be discovered in the waters off Cornwall. In fact, the area is known for being a graveyard of ships, with hundreds of vessels having sunk in the treacherous waters over the centuries. The discovery of the other wreck also highlighted the challenges of identifying shipwrecks, as many ships from the same period carried similar cargoes and were built using similar designs. Even with modern technology, it can be difficult to definitively identify a wreck without finding key artifacts or records that can link it to a specific ship.

The treasure of the *Merchant Royal* continues to capture the imaginations of treasure hunters and adventurers. Some believe that the wreck lies buried deep beneath layers of sand and silt, hidden from view by the ocean's ever-shifting currents. Others think that the treasure may have been scattered across the seabed when the ship sank, with pieces of gold and silver lying in small pockets across a wide area. There are even rumors that some of the treasure may have been recovered shortly after the sinking by fishermen or local divers, though there is no concrete evidence to support these claims.

The search for the *Merchant Royal* has also raised questions about the ethics of treasure hunting and the ownership of historical artifacts. The ship was carrying treasure that belonged to the Spanish crown, and if the wreck were to be found, there would likely be legal disputes over who has the right to claim the treasure. Spain, as the original owner of the gold and silver, could make a case for its return, while England, as the country where the ship sank, could also have a claim. In recent years, there has been growing concern about the looting of shipwrecks and the need to protect underwater cultural heritage from exploitation.

Despite these challenges, the allure of the *Merchant Royal* and its hidden treasure remains as strong as ever. The idea of a fortune in gold and silver lying at the bottom of the ocean, waiting to be discovered, continues to inspire dreams of adventure and riches. For treasure hunters, the *Merchant Royal* represents the ultimate prize—a lost shipwreck carrying one of the largest treasures ever lost at sea. And for historians and archaeologists, the wreck holds the promise of uncovering new insights into the maritime history of the 17th century and the complex web of trade, politics, and conflict that defined the era.

The story of the *Merchant Royal* is a reminder of the dangers and uncertainties of life at sea during the Age of Sail. Ships like the *Merchant Royal* were at the mercy of the elements, and even the most experienced captains and crews could find themselves facing disaster in the unpredictable waters of the Atlantic. The loss of the *Merchant Royal* and its treasure is one of the great maritime tragedies of the 17th century, but it is also a story of resilience and determination. The crew of the *Merchant Royal* fought bravely to save their ship, and even in the face of certain disaster, they managed to escape with their lives.

As the search for the *Merchant Royal* continues, new technologies and techniques may one day unlock the secrets of the lost ship and its hidden gold. Until then, the legend of the *Merchant Royal* will live on, a tantalizing mystery that keeps adventurers and historians dreaming of the day when the treasure is finally brought to the surface. Whether or not the wreck is ever found, the story of the *Merchant Royal* and its lost treasure will continue to captivate the imagination for generations to come.

Chapter 17: The Shipwrecks of Cape Horn

Cape Horn, located at the southernmost tip of South America, is infamous for its treacherous seas, violent storms, and unpredictable weather, earning it the reputation of being one of the most dangerous shipping routes in the world. For centuries, sailors feared Cape Horn, as it claimed the lives of thousands of seamen and sent countless ships to a watery grave. Known as a graveyard for ships, the waters around Cape Horn have been the final resting place for hundreds of vessels, and the shipwrecks of Cape Horn remain one of the most tragic and fascinating maritime mysteries of all time.

The story of Cape Horn begins in the early 17th century when European explorers and traders were searching for new trade routes between Europe, the Americas, and the East Indies. At the time, ships traveling from Europe to Asia or the west coast of the Americas had to navigate around the southern tip of South America to avoid the narrow and dangerous Strait of Magellan, which was difficult to navigate due to its sharp turns and unpredictable currents. The Dutch explorer Willem Schouten was the first to round Cape Horn in 1616, opening a new route that would become one of the busiest shipping lanes in the world.

However, rounding Cape Horn was no easy task. The waters at the confluence of the Atlantic and Pacific Oceans are some of the roughest in the world. The meeting of these two powerful oceans creates a constant battle of strong winds, towering waves, and sudden storms. These storms can strike without warning, bringing hurricane-force winds, freezing temperatures, and waves that can reach heights of 50 feet or more. In addition, the strong currents and hidden underwater rocks make navigation extremely difficult. Even the most experienced sailors found it nearly impossible to predict the weather around Cape

Horn, and many ships that attempted to round the cape were caught in deadly storms and never seen again.

During the 18th and 19th centuries, Cape Horn became a vital route for ships involved in global trade. As European empires expanded their colonies and trade networks, ships carrying valuable cargo such as spices, textiles, precious metals, and manufactured goods regularly sailed around Cape Horn on their way to the East Indies, China, and the west coast of the Americas. At the same time, whaling and sealing ships made the dangerous voyage to the rich waters of the Southern Ocean, where they hunted for whales and seals, whose oil and fur were highly prized commodities. However, the booming trade around Cape Horn came at a heavy cost.

The constant storms and rough seas around Cape Horn created a deadly environment for ships. Many vessels were caught in the powerful storms and thrown against the rocky coastline, where they broke apart and sank. Others were damaged by the violent waves and strong winds, which tore apart their sails, snapped their masts, and left them adrift, helpless in the vast and unforgiving ocean. For every successful voyage around Cape Horn, there were countless tragedies, and shipwrecks became a common occurrence.

One of the most famous shipwrecks near Cape Horn occurred in 1852 when the *Lord Raglan*, a British ship carrying passengers and cargo, encountered a massive storm while attempting to round the cape. The storm was so severe that it caused the ship to capsize, sending the vessel and its passengers into the icy waters. Only a handful of survivors were rescued, and the wreck of the *Lord Raglan* became one of the many tragic tales of lost ships in the Cape Horn region. Stories like this one were common, as many ships were unable to withstand the brutal conditions of the Southern Ocean.

Another tragic shipwreck that occurred near Cape Horn was that of the *Deutschland*, a German vessel that sank in 1875. The ship was caught in a violent storm while rounding the cape and was pushed onto the rocks by the powerful waves. The crew attempted to save the ship by lowering lifeboats, but the icy water and strong currents made it impossible to reach safety. Most of the crew perished in the wreck, and the few survivors who managed to reach the shore were stranded on the desolate and inhospitable landscape of Tierra del Fuego, where they were forced to survive in freezing temperatures with little food or shelter.

One of the reasons why Cape Horn was so deadly for ships was the extreme weather conditions of the Southern Ocean. The latitude of Cape Horn, at around 56 degrees south, places it in the "roaring forties" and "furious fifties"—regions of the Southern Hemisphere known for their strong westerly winds that can blow nonstop for thousands of miles. These winds, combined with the powerful currents of the Southern Ocean, create the perfect conditions for massive storms. The cold waters of the Antarctic Ocean, which lie just to the south of Cape Horn, also contribute to the harsh conditions, as freezing temperatures and icebergs add an additional layer of danger for ships trying to navigate the cape.

In addition to the violent storms and rough seas, the geography of Cape Horn itself posed significant challenges for ships. The southern tip of South America is dotted with numerous islands, rocky outcroppings, and narrow channels that make navigation extremely difficult, especially in poor weather. The hidden underwater rocks and shallow waters near the coastline made it easy for ships to run aground or be pushed onto the rocks by the strong winds and currents. Even ships that managed to survive the storms could be dashed against the rocky cliffs or break apart on the shallow reefs.

The perilous conditions of Cape Horn earned it the nickname "Sailor's Graveyard." It became a rite of passage for sailors to round Cape Horn, and those who survived the treacherous journey were often regarded as heroes. Many sailors referred to Cape Horn as the "End of the World" because it was the last obstacle between them and the vast, open waters of the Southern Ocean. The dangers of Cape Horn were so great that many sailors refused to make the journey, and some shipping companies even offered higher wages to crews willing to brave the deadly waters.

Despite the dangers, ships continued to round Cape Horn throughout the 19th century, as it remained a vital route for global trade. The discovery of gold in California in 1848 and the subsequent Gold Rush led to a massive increase in shipping traffic around Cape Horn, as ships carrying prospectors, supplies, and equipment made the long journey from the East Coast of the United States to California. At the same time, ships carrying valuable cargo from Europe and the East Indies continued to pass through the region. However, the increase in traffic also led to more shipwrecks, as more and more vessels were lost to the deadly waters of Cape Horn.

One of the most tragic shipwrecks of the Gold Rush era occurred in 1857 when the *Jabez Howes*, an American ship carrying gold prospectors and their supplies, sank near Cape Horn during a storm. The ship was caught in a violent gale, and despite the crew's efforts to keep the vessel afloat, it was eventually overcome by the powerful waves. The ship sank with all hands on board, and the gold prospectors' dreams of fortune were lost along with the ship. The wreck of the *Jabez Howes* became yet another tragic chapter in the long history of shipwrecks around Cape Horn.

The late 19th and early 20th centuries saw the development of steam-powered ships, which began to replace the traditional sailing vessels that had been used for centuries. Steamships were more powerful and less reliant on the wind, allowing them to navigate more easily around Cape Horn. However, even steam-powered ships were not immune to the dangers of the region. In 1905, the British steamship *Scotsman* was caught in a fierce storm near Cape Horn and was driven onto the rocks. Despite the ship's modern technology, it was unable to withstand the power of the storm, and the crew was forced to abandon ship. The wreck of the *Scotsman* became one of the last major shipwrecks in the region before the opening of the Panama Canal in 1914.

The construction of the Panama Canal marked the beginning of the end for Cape Horn as a major shipping route. The canal provided a safer and faster route for ships traveling between the Atlantic and Pacific Oceans, eliminating the need to round the dangerous waters of Cape Horn. As a result, the number of ships passing through the region declined dramatically, and with it, the number of shipwrecks. However, the legacy of Cape Horn's shipwrecks lives on, and the wrecks that lie at the bottom of the ocean are a testament to the bravery and determination of the sailors who attempted to navigate one of the world's most dangerous maritime routes.

Today, the shipwrecks of Cape Horn remain a popular subject of study for marine archaeologists and historians. The wrecks provide a window into the past, offering valuable insights into the ships and sailors who braved the treacherous waters of the Southern Ocean. Many of the wrecks have been preserved by the cold waters of the region, and some have been explored by underwater archaeologists using advanced technology such as sonar and remotely operated vehicles (ROVs). The exploration of these wrecks has revealed fascinating artifacts, including personal items, cargo, and even the remains of the ships themselves, all of which provide a glimpse into the lives of the sailors who once sailed these deadly waters.

The shipwrecks of Cape Horn are also a source of fascination for treasure hunters and adventurers. Many of the ships that sank in the region were carrying valuable cargo, including gold, silver, and other precious goods. While some of this treasure has been recovered over the years, much of it remains lost at the bottom of the ocean, waiting to be discovered. The lure of hidden treasure continues to draw adventurers to the region, and the search for the lost riches of Cape Horn remains an enduring mystery.

In addition to the shipwrecks themselves, the stories of the sailors who braved Cape Horn continue to captivate the imagination. The tales of courage, determination, and tragedy that surround the shipwrecks of Cape Horn are a testament to the resilience of the human spirit in the face of overwhelming odds. Whether it's the story of the brave crew of the *Lord Raglan*, who fought to the bitter end against the storm, or the tragic fate of the *Deutschland*, whose crew perished in the freezing waters, these stories remind us of the dangers of the sea and the strength of those who dared to challenge it.

Though the era of sailing ships has long passed, the shipwrecks of Cape Horn remain as a haunting reminder of the perils of the sea. Today, modern ships equipped with advanced navigation technology and weather forecasting tools can safely bypass Cape Horn by using the Panama Canal. But for the sailors of the past, Cape Horn represented the ultimate test of their skill and courage. The shipwrecks that lie scattered across the ocean floor are a testament to their struggle and sacrifice, and their stories will continue to be told for generations to come.

Chapter 18: The Curse of the Nuestra Señora de Atocha

The tale of the *Nuestra Señora de Atocha* is one of the most famous and intriguing stories of sunken treasure, tragedy, and mystery in maritime history. This Spanish galleon, laden with gold, silver, and precious jewels, met its untimely fate in the treacherous waters of the Florida Keys in 1622. The *Atocha*'s incredible wealth, combined with its tragic sinking and the centuries-long search to recover its treasure, has captivated treasure hunters and historians alike. But what makes the story even more fascinating is the supposed curse that some believe haunts the ship and those who dare to seek its fortune. The legend of the *Nuestra Señora de Atocha* has grown over the years, weaving together elements of history, mystery, and the supernatural.

In the early 17th century, Spain was one of the most powerful nations in the world, largely due to its vast overseas empire. Spanish ships frequently sailed between the Americas and Europe, transporting enormous amounts of gold, silver, and other valuable goods from the New World to Spain. These treasures, collected from the mines of Peru, Mexico, and Bolivia, were vital to Spain's economy, which relied heavily on the wealth generated by its colonies. The Spanish crown tightly controlled this trade, organizing fleets of ships called "treasure fleets" to protect the valuable cargo from pirates, storms, and other dangers.

The *Nuestra Señora de Atocha* was part of one such fleet. She was a heavily armed galleon, built to defend against the constant threat of pirates that roamed the Caribbean. In 1622, the *Atocha* was loaded with an extraordinary cargo of treasure bound for Spain. Her cargo holds were filled with silver coins, gold bars, emeralds, copper, and other precious goods. In total, the ship was carrying an estimated 40 tons of treasure, making it one of the richest ships to ever sail from the Americas.

However, the *Atocha*'s journey would end in disaster. On September 6, 1622, the treasure fleet, which included the *Atocha*, set sail from Havana, Cuba, bound for Spain. The fleet hoped to make a quick and safe journey across the Atlantic before the hurricane season reached its peak. But just two days after departing Havana, the fleet was caught in a massive hurricane as it passed through the Florida Straits. The winds and waves were relentless, and the ships were no match for the ferocity of the storm.

The *Atocha* and several other ships in the fleet were driven onto the reefs near the Florida Keys, where they were battered by the powerful waves. The *Atocha* struck a reef and began to take on water rapidly. Despite the efforts of the crew to save the ship, it quickly sank to the ocean floor. Of the 265 people aboard the *Atocha*, only five survived—three crew members and two slaves—who managed to cling to the ship's rigging as the vessel sank beneath the waves. The rest of the passengers and crew perished in the storm, their bodies lost to the sea along with the ship's precious cargo.

In the aftermath of the disaster, the Spanish government immediately began efforts to recover the lost treasure. Divers were sent to the wreck site to retrieve the valuable cargo, but their efforts were hampered by the treacherous waters, strong currents, and the depth at which the ship lay. Although some treasure was recovered from the shallow waters near the wreck, the majority of the *Atocha*'s fortune remained lost, buried beneath layers of sand and coral on the ocean floor. Over time, the wreck of the *Atocha* was forgotten, and it became one of the greatest lost treasures in history.

For centuries, treasure hunters have been drawn to the legend of the *Atocha*. Many believed that the ship's cargo still lay hidden beneath the waters of the Florida Keys, waiting to be discovered. But the search for the *Atocha* would prove to be incredibly difficult. The area where the ship sank is known for its treacherous conditions, with strong currents, shifting sands, and dangerous reefs making it nearly impossible to locate the wreck. In addition, the wreck had been scattered by the force of the hurricane, and much of the treasure was buried deep in the seabed, hidden from view.

Despite these challenges, the allure of the *Atocha's* treasure continued to attract adventurers. Over the years, numerous attempts were made to locate the wreck, but all ended in failure. Many believed that the treasure was cursed, and that anyone who tried to find it would meet with disaster. According to legend, the *Atocha* was protected by a curse placed on it by the spirits of the sailors and passengers who perished in the storm. Some treasure hunters claimed to have experienced strange and eerie occurrences while searching for the wreck, including sudden storms, mysterious accidents, and unexplained deaths.

The most famous attempt to locate the *Atocha* came in the 20th century, when American treasure hunter Mel Fisher took up the search. Fisher, a former chicken farmer and diving enthusiast, became obsessed with the idea of finding the *Atocha* after learning about the ship's incredible treasure. In 1969, Fisher and his team began their quest to locate the wreck, spending years scouring the waters of the Florida Keys for any sign of the lost ship. They faced numerous setbacks along the way, including financial difficulties, legal battles, and even personal tragedy. Fisher's son, Dirk, and his daughter-in-law were killed in a diving accident while searching for the wreck, further fueling the belief that the *Atocha* was cursed.

Despite these hardships, Fisher refused to give up. He and his team continued their search, using advanced technology such as sonar and metal detectors to comb the ocean floor for clues. For years, they found only small fragments of the wreck—pieces of wood, cannonballs, and other debris—but the main treasure eluded them. Then, in 1985, after more than 16 years of searching, Fisher's persistence finally paid off. His team discovered the main wreck site of the *Atocha*, along with its incredible cargo of treasure.

The discovery was one of the most significant finds in the history of treasure hunting. Fisher and his team recovered an estimated $400 million worth of gold, silver, emeralds, and other precious items from the wreck. Among the most valuable finds were thousands of silver coins, hundreds of gold bars, and a collection of stunning emeralds, including one of the largest emeralds ever discovered. The treasure was so vast that it took years to fully recover and catalog everything that had been found.

Despite the excitement of the discovery, the legend of the *Atocha*'s curse continued to haunt Fisher and his team. Some claimed that the curse had been responsible for the many difficulties Fisher faced during his search, including the tragic loss of his son. Others believed that the curse had been lifted once the treasure was found, and that the spirits of the ship's crew and passengers had finally been laid to rest. Fisher himself, however, dismissed the idea of a curse, attributing the challenges he faced to the dangers and unpredictability of treasure hunting.

The recovery of the *Atocha*'s treasure sparked a legal battle between Fisher and the state of Florida, which claimed ownership of the treasure since it had been found in Florida waters. Fisher fought the claim, arguing that the treasure rightfully belonged to him and his team, who had spent years and millions of dollars searching for it. The case eventually went to the U.S. Supreme Court, which ruled in Fisher's favor, allowing him to keep the treasure. This legal victory was a major milestone in the history of treasure hunting and set a precedent for future cases involving sunken treasure.

Even after Fisher's discovery, the legend of the *Atocha* and its curse continued to grow. Some treasure hunters believe that there is still more treasure to be found, as historical records suggest that the *Atocha* was carrying even more gold and silver than what was recovered. Fisher's team found only about half of the estimated cargo, leading some to speculate that the rest of the treasure may still be hidden beneath the ocean floor, waiting to be discovered. The search for the remaining treasure continues to this day, with modern treasure hunters using advanced technology to explore the waters around the wreck site.

The *Atocha* has also become a symbol of both the risks and rewards of treasure hunting. The dangers faced by those who seek lost treasure—whether from natural elements, legal challenges, or personal tragedy—are very real, and the story of the *Atocha* serves as a reminder of the high cost of pursuing such a dream. Yet, for those who are willing to take the risk, the potential rewards are equally great. The discovery of the *Atocha* was one of the most spectacular finds in maritime history, and it continues to inspire adventurers to this day.

The treasure of the *Nuestra Señora de Atocha* is now displayed in museums and private collections, allowing people from around the world to marvel at the incredible wealth that was once lost to the sea. The emeralds, gold bars, and silver coins recovered from the wreck are a testament to the riches of the Spanish Empire and the daring voyages that brought those treasures across the Atlantic. For historians, the wreck of the *Atocha* provides valuable insights into the maritime history of the 17th century, including the trade routes, shipbuilding techniques, and cultural exchanges that defined the era.

For those who believe in the supernatural, the legend of the *Atocha*'s curse continues to add an element of mystery to the story. Whether or not the curse is real, the challenges and tragedies faced by those who sought the treasure cannot be denied. The *Atocha* remains one of the most famous and mysterious shipwrecks in history, a symbol of both human ambition and the untamed power of the sea.

Chapter 19: The Mystery of the SS Waratah

The SS *Waratah* is one of the most haunting mysteries of the sea, a ship that simply vanished without a trace, leaving behind no wreckage, no survivors, and no definitive explanation. The mystery of the *Waratah* has fascinated historians, maritime experts, and adventurers for over a century, and even today, the story remains one of the ocean's most enduring unsolved enigmas.

The SS *Waratah* was a passenger and cargo steamship, built in 1908 by Barclay, Curle & Co. Ltd in Glasgow, Scotland. She was designed to travel between Europe and Australia, a time when sea travel was the primary means of long-distance transportation. The *Waratah* was a large vessel for her time, measuring 465 feet long and weighing over 9,300 tons. She was meant to be a luxurious ship, offering wealthy passengers the comforts of modern travel during the long voyage across the Indian Ocean. With elegant dining rooms, lavish cabins, and comfortable lounges, the *Waratah* promised to be a grand experience for those aboard.

The ship was named after the Waratah, a beautiful red flower native to Australia, and she was intended to symbolize the growing connection between Britain and its far-flung colony. The *Waratah* was part of the Blue Anchor Line, a shipping company that specialized in routes between Britain and Australia, carrying both passengers and cargo. At first, she seemed to perform well, completing her maiden voyage from London to Sydney with no major issues. However, there were whispers of trouble from some passengers and crew members even before her ill-fated final voyage. There were reports that the *Waratah* was a bit top-heavy, meaning that the ship might not be as stable as it should have been in rough seas.

On her second voyage, in July 1909, the *Waratah* set out from Durban, South Africa, heading toward Cape Town. This was part of her long journey back to Britain. On board were 211 passengers and crew, along with a valuable cargo of goods including wool, meat, and gold. Among the passengers were businessmen, tourists, and even some notable individuals, all making the journey between continents. As the ship left Durban, everything seemed normal. The weather was fair, and there were no immediate signs of trouble. But as the *Waratah* sailed farther into the Indian Ocean, something went terribly wrong.

The *Waratah* was last seen on July 27, 1909, by the crew of another ship, the SS *Clan MacIntyre*. The *Clan MacIntyre* reported that the *Waratah* was sailing smoothly about 9 miles off the coast of South Africa, near the notorious stretch of water known as the Wild Coast. The Wild Coast is infamous for its dangerous seas, with powerful currents, sudden storms, and massive swells that can overwhelm even the sturdiest ships. However, there was no indication at the time that the *Waratah* was in any immediate danger. After that sighting, the *Waratah* simply disappeared.

When the *Waratah* failed to arrive in Cape Town as scheduled, there was immediate concern. The ship was carrying dozens of passengers and crew, along with valuable cargo, and any delay was unusual. Days turned into weeks, and still there was no word from the ship. Rescue efforts were launched, with search parties scouring the seas between Durban and Cape Town, but no trace of the *Waratah* was ever found. There was no wreckage, no lifeboats, no bodies—nothing to suggest what had happened to the ship or its occupants. It was as if the *Waratah* had been swallowed by the ocean.

The disappearance of the *Waratah* quickly became one of the greatest maritime mysteries of the time. Theories about what had happened to the ship began to circulate, but none could be proven. Some believed that the *Waratah* had encountered a sudden and violent storm, which had caused the top-heavy ship to capsize and sink rapidly.

The Wild Coast, with its unpredictable weather and rough seas, was a known hazard for ships, and it seemed plausible that a storm could have overwhelmed the *Waratah* before she had a chance to send out a distress signal. However, without any wreckage or survivors, this theory remained speculative.

Others suggested that the ship had experienced some sort of mechanical failure or fire, which had led to her sinking. The *Waratah* was carrying a large amount of coal in her bunkers, and it was possible that a fire had broken out below deck, causing an explosion or structural damage. Again, there was no evidence to support this idea, but it remained one of many possible explanations. Some experts also considered the possibility of human error, suggesting that the ship's captain or crew may have made a navigational mistake, steering the vessel into dangerous waters or reefs that caused her to sink.

As the years passed, the mystery deepened. Despite numerous search efforts, including expeditions launched by both private individuals and the government, the wreck of the *Waratah* was never found. This lack of evidence only fueled more fantastical theories. Some people speculated that the ship had fallen victim to a rogue wave, a massive wall of water capable of sinking even large vessels. Rogue waves, while rare, are known to occur in the open ocean and can strike without warning. Given the treacherous waters of the Wild Coast, this theory seemed plausible to some.

Other, more outlandish ideas emerged as well. Some people claimed that the *Waratah* had been attacked by pirates or that it had been deliberately sabotaged by someone on board. These theories were never taken seriously by maritime experts, but they added to the air of mystery surrounding the ship's disappearance. There were also stories of ghostly sightings of the *Waratah*, with sailors and fishermen reporting that they had seen the ship sailing in the distance, only for it to vanish before their eyes. These ghost ship stories added a supernatural element to the mystery, with some believing that the *Waratah* was cursed or that it had entered another dimension, never to return.

One of the more interesting aspects of the *Waratah* mystery is the testimony of a man named Claude Sawyer, a passenger who disembarked from the ship in Durban just before its final voyage. Sawyer claimed to have had a premonition that something terrible was going to happen to the *Waratah*, and he was so disturbed by his visions that he decided to leave the ship and continue his journey on land. After the ship disappeared, Sawyer's story gained attention, and many wondered if he had truly foreseen the ship's doom. Some believe that Sawyer's premonition was just a coincidence, while others think that it may have been an eerie warning of the tragedy to come.

In the years following the disappearance, several expeditions were launched to locate the wreck of the *Waratah*. In 1910, a search effort led by the British Admiralty scoured the waters along the ship's intended route, but no trace of the vessel was found. In the decades that followed, numerous attempts were made to find the wreck using more advanced technology, including sonar and deep-sea exploration equipment. Despite these efforts, the *Waratah* has remained elusive, with no definitive evidence of the ship's resting place.

In recent years, some tantalizing clues have emerged that suggest the wreck of the *Waratah* may finally be within reach. In the early 2000s, marine explorers discovered what appeared to be a large, sunken ship off the coast of South Africa, in an area consistent with the *Waratah*'s last known location. However, the wreck was too deep to be properly examined at the time, and further expeditions were needed to confirm whether or not the ship was indeed the *Waratah*. Despite these promising leads, the mystery remains unsolved, and the exact fate of the *Waratah* and her passengers continues to be debated.

One of the reasons the *Waratah*'s disappearance has remained such a compelling mystery is the complete lack of physical evidence. In most cases of shipwrecks, even if the ship itself is lost, debris such as lifeboats, personal belongings, or cargo will wash ashore. In the case of the *Waratah*, however, no such debris was ever found, leading some to speculate that the ship may have sunk very quickly, possibly due to a catastrophic failure or violent event that left no time for the crew or passengers to react.

The story of the *Waratah* has become part of maritime folklore, a cautionary tale about the dangers of the sea and the unpredictability of the ocean. For the families of those who were lost, the mystery is a painful reminder of the fragility of life at sea. Many descendants of the passengers and crew still hold out hope that one day the wreck will be found, and that the final moments of the *Waratah* will be understood. Until then, the ship's fate remains one of the ocean's most enduring mysteries.

The SS *Waratah* has also become a symbol of the unknown—the vast and often unexplored depths of the ocean, where ships can disappear without a trace, swallowed by the deep blue sea. Whether the *Waratah* met her end in a storm, a rogue wave, or some other disaster, her story continues to intrigue and inspire. Modern technology has brought us closer to solving many of the ocean's mysteries, but the *Waratah* reminds us that the sea still holds many secrets, waiting to be discovered by those brave enough to seek them out.

Chapter 20: Unsolved Secrets of the Ocean Depths

The ocean is one of the most mysterious and unexplored places on Earth, covering more than 70% of our planet's surface and holding secrets that stretch back millions of years. While we have mapped out parts of the land and even ventured into space, the ocean depths remain largely unknown, a dark and alien world where strange creatures thrive and ancient shipwrecks lie forgotten. Scientists believe that we have explored less than 5% of the ocean, meaning that most of this vast underwater world is still a mystery. Within its cold, black depths lie unsolved secrets that have puzzled scientists, explorers, and adventurers for centuries.

One of the most intriguing mysteries of the ocean depths is the existence of strange and unidentifiable sounds. Over the years, deep-sea microphones called hydrophones have picked up various eerie sounds that defy explanation. One of the most famous is known as the "Bloop." First detected in 1997, the Bloop was an incredibly loud, low-frequency sound that was heard by sensors more than 3,000 miles apart. The sound was so powerful that it suggested something massive—perhaps even larger than a blue whale, the largest known animal on Earth—was responsible for it. At first, some speculated that the sound could have come from a previously unknown sea creature living deep in the ocean. However, no such creature has ever been discovered, and scientists eventually suggested that the Bloop might have been caused by the cracking of icebergs. Despite this explanation, the mystery lingers, with many still wondering if some colossal, undiscovered sea monster could be lurking in the depths.

Another mystery that has fascinated people for years is the existence of the so-called "ocean UFOs," or Unidentified Submerged Objects (USOs). These are mysterious objects that have been spotted moving rapidly beneath the water, sometimes at speeds that seem impossible for any known marine vehicle or animal. Sightings of USOs have been reported by sailors, fishermen, and even naval personnel, who describe strange, glowing lights or fast-moving shapes darting through the water. Some believe these sightings are evidence of advanced underwater technology, possibly created by extraterrestrial beings. Others think that they could be top-secret military experiments or even natural phenomena that we don't yet understand. However, the true nature of these USOs remains unknown, adding to the list of unsolved secrets hidden beneath the waves.

The deep ocean is also home to countless shipwrecks, some of which have been lost for centuries. While many famous shipwrecks, such as the *Titanic*, have been located, there are still countless vessels that have disappeared without a trace, their wreckage lying somewhere on the ocean floor. One of the most legendary of these lost ships is the *Flor de la Mar*, a Portuguese galleon that sank off the coast of Sumatra in 1511. The *Flor de la Mar* was reportedly carrying a vast treasure, including gold, silver, and precious jewels, making it one of the most valuable shipwrecks in history. Despite numerous searches, the wreck of the *Flor de la Mar* has never been found, and its treasure remains one of the greatest unsolved mysteries of the ocean.

Another famous lost ship is the USS *Cyclops*, which vanished in 1918 while sailing through the Bermuda Triangle. The *Cyclops* was a large U.S. Navy ship, and its disappearance remains one of the biggest mysteries of the Bermuda Triangle, an area notorious for the unexplained vanishings of ships and planes. The *Cyclops* was carrying more than 300 people when it disappeared, and no distress signal was ever sent. Despite extensive search efforts, no wreckage or survivors were ever found, leading to numerous theories about what might have happened to the ship. Some believe that the *Cyclops* may have been sunk by a rogue wave, while others speculate that it was pulled into an underwater vortex or even abducted by extraterrestrials. The Bermuda

Triangle itself is one of the most enduring ocean mysteries, with dozens of ships and planes having disappeared in the area over the years.

The mysteries of the ocean are not limited to human-made objects, however. The deep sea is home to some of the most bizarre and unknown creatures on the planet. Scientists estimate that there may be millions of species living in the ocean that have yet to be discovered. One of the most mysterious deep-sea creatures is the giant squid, which was once thought to be a mythical sea monster. While we now know that giant squids do exist, they are rarely seen and live at depths that make them difficult to study. Even more elusive is the colossal squid, which is even larger than the giant squid and may grow up to 46 feet long. These massive creatures have been the inspiration for many sea monster legends, including tales of the kraken, a giant, ship-destroying squid from Norse mythology. Despite advances in deep-sea exploration, much about these creatures remains unknown, including how they behave, reproduce, and hunt in the pitch-black waters of the deep ocean.

In addition to these giant squids, the ocean depths are home to a range of strange and otherworldly creatures, many of which have evolved unique adaptations to survive in the extreme conditions of the deep sea. These animals live in complete darkness, where the pressure is so intense that it would crush most surface-dwelling creatures. Yet, they have developed incredible ways to thrive in this harsh environment. Some, like the anglerfish, have bioluminescent lures that glow in the dark to attract prey. Others, like the gulper eel, have enormous mouths that allow them to swallow prey much larger than themselves. Even more bizarre are the "zombie worms," which survive by feeding on the bones of dead whales that have sunk to the ocean floor. These creatures are so strange and alien that they seem to belong to another world, yet they are very much a part of the ocean's mysterious and unexplored depths.

Another unsolved mystery of the ocean is the existence of underwater ruins and lost civilizations. One of the most famous of these is the legend of Atlantis, an advanced civilization that supposedly sank beneath the ocean thousands of years ago. While Atlantis is generally considered to be a myth, there are real underwater ruins that have been discovered in various parts of the world. One of the most remarkable of these is the sunken city of Dwarka, off the coast of India. Archaeologists have found evidence of an ancient city submerged beneath the waves, which some believe could be the legendary city of Dwarka, mentioned in Hindu mythology as the kingdom of Lord Krishna. The ruins contain stone structures, pottery, and other artifacts that suggest the city was once a thriving metropolis, but how and why it ended up underwater remains a mystery.

Similarly, in Japan, off the coast of Yonaguni Island, a mysterious underwater structure known as the Yonaguni Monument was discovered in the 1980s. The monument consists of massive stone formations that resemble steps, terraces, and walls, leading some to speculate that it is the remains of an ancient, unknown civilization. However, there is still debate among experts about whether the Yonaguni Monument is man-made or simply a natural formation created by the ocean's currents and geological activity. If it is man-made, it could provide evidence of a lost civilization that existed long before recorded history, adding yet another layer of mystery to the ocean's depths.

In addition to ancient ruins, the ocean holds the secrets of countless sunken planes and military vessels. One of the most puzzling unsolved mysteries involves the disappearance of Malaysian Airlines Flight MH370, which vanished in 2014 while flying over the Indian Ocean. Despite extensive search efforts involving dozens of countries, the plane's wreckage was never found, and the fate of the 239 people on board remains a heartbreaking and perplexing mystery. The vastness of the ocean, combined with the difficulty of searching its depths, has made finding the plane's wreckage incredibly challenging, and the story of MH370 continues to baffle experts and families to this day.

The ocean's depths also hold evidence of past natural disasters, such as underwater volcanic eruptions, tsunamis, and massive landslides. These events can create dramatic changes in the ocean's landscape and may even leave behind clues about the history of Earth's climate and geology. For example, scientists studying the ocean floor have found evidence of a massive underwater landslide that occurred off the coast of Norway around 8,000 years ago. Known as the Storegga Slide, this event caused a huge tsunami that likely wiped out coastal communities in northern Europe. By studying these underwater geological events, scientists hope to learn more about the history of our planet and possibly predict future natural disasters.

Perhaps one of the greatest mysteries of the ocean depths is the search for extraterrestrial life. While space is often considered the final frontier, some scientists believe that the ocean could hold clues to the existence of life beyond Earth. The deep sea is home to extreme environments, such as hydrothermal vents, where life thrives without sunlight, relying instead on chemicals released by the Earth's crust. These extreme conditions are similar to those found on other planets and moons, such as Europa, one of Jupiter's moons, which is believed to have a subsurface ocean beneath its icy surface. By studying the life forms that exist in these harsh environments on Earth, scientists hope to better understand the possibility of life elsewhere in the universe.

As technology advances, we are slowly beginning to unlock some of the ocean's secrets. Submersibles, remotely operated vehicles (ROVs), and underwater drones are allowing us to explore deeper than ever before. These technologies have led to amazing discoveries, from new species of deep-sea creatures to ancient shipwrecks and lost cities. Yet, despite these advances, the ocean remains a largely uncharted and mysterious realm, with countless secrets still waiting to be uncovered.

The unsolved mysteries of the ocean depths continue to captivate our imaginations. From strange sounds and ghost ships to undiscovered creatures and lost civilizations, the ocean holds the potential for endless discovery. Each new exploration brings us closer to understanding this vast and enigmatic world, but with so much left to explore, the ocean will likely remain a source of wonder and mystery for generations to come. The secrets of the deep may never be fully solved, but that only adds to the allure of this vast, hidden frontier.

Epilogue

Our journey across the vast and mysterious ocean has come to an end—for now. Together, we've uncovered the stories of ships that vanished, treasures that were lost, and legends that have been whispered through generations. The ocean, with its endless waves and mysterious depths, is a place of wonder where the past and present intertwine, keeping secrets hidden just beneath the surface.

While some mysteries were solved, many remain unanswered. Why did certain ships disappear without a trace? What truly happened to the treasures lost at sea? The ocean holds these secrets close, reminding us that there is still so much left to explore and understand. And that's what makes it so special—it leaves room for curiosity, imagination, and adventure.

As you close this book, remember that the stories we've uncovered are just a glimpse of what lies beneath the waves. The ocean is still full of unsolved puzzles waiting for explorers like you to discover. Who knows—maybe one day you'll set sail on your own adventure, find a hidden treasure, or even solve a mystery that has puzzled people for centuries.

The sea will always call to those who listen closely, and the mysteries of the deep will continue to inspire new explorers to chase after the unknown. So, hold onto your sense of wonder and adventure, because the ocean's greatest mysteries are never truly over. They are out there, somewhere, waiting for the next brave adventurer to uncover them.

Until then, fair winds and following seas, young explorer. The adventure is just beginning.

The End.

Milton Keynes UK
Ingram Content Group UK Ltd.
UKHW020758231024
450026UK00001B/97

9 798227 378064